Educators at the Bargaining Table

Educators at the Bargaining Table

Successfully Negotiating a Contract That Works for All

Todd A. DeMitchell

ROWMAN & LITTLEFIELD
Lanham · Boulder · New York · London

Published by Rowman & Littlefield
A wholly owned subsidiary of The Rowman & Littlefield Publishing Group, Inc.
4501 Forbes Boulevard, Suite 200, Lanham, Maryland 20706
www.rowman.com

Unit A, Whitacre Mews, 26–34 Stannary Street, London SE11 4AB

British Library Cataloguing in Publication Information Available

Library of Congress Cataloging-in-Publication Data
Names: DeMitchell, Todd A, author.
Title: Educators at the bargaining table : successfully negotiating a contract that works for all / Todd A. DeMitchell.
Description: Lanham : Rowman & Littlfield, [2017] | Includes bibliographical references.
Identifiers: LCCN 2017059800 (print) | LCCN 2018001000 (ebook) |
   ISBN 9781475808087 (Electronic) | ISBN 9781475808063 (cloth : alk. paper) |
   ISBN 9781475808070 (pbk. : alk. paper)
Subjects: LCSH: Collective bargaining—Teachers.
Classification: LCC LB2844.58 (ebook) | LCC LB2844.58 .D45 2017 (print) |
   DDC 331.88/113711—dc23
LC record available at https://lccn.loc.gov/2017059800

♾™ The paper used in this publication meets the minimum requirements of American National Standard for Information Sciences—Permanence of Paper for Printed Library Materials, ANSI/NISO Z39.48–1992.

Printed in the United States of America

Contents

Preface

Few educators actually sit at the bargaining table, but all educators in a school district are impacted by the outcome of what occurs at the bargaining table. Wages, benefits, and terms and conditions of employment are decided at the table. Issues such as what is my salary, what are my benefits, what are my job responsibilities, and what security do I have in my employment are hammered out at that table. What happens at the table is important and does not stay at the table.

Educators at the Bargaining Table: Successfully Negotiating a Contract That Works for All is based on the prior 2010 *Labor Relations in Education: Policy, Politics, and Practices* (Rowman & Littlefield). Since January 2010 a lot has happened in educational labor relations. While the call up to 2010 was to reform unions and labor relations, since that time, the word reform has taken on a distinctly different meaning.

Tenure has been under siege in the courts, as well as in legislative halls, seeking to make it easier to fire teachers. The scope of bargaining has been narrowed. A starve-the-beast approach regarding dues deductions has been implemented in many states. Agency fees have faced court challenges, and a number of states passed right-to-work legislation allowing employees covered by a collective bargaining agreement (CBA) to opt out of paying a fee to the union for their bargaining and enforcement of the contract.

These changes and challenges to teacher unions and labor relations, in general, prompted a review of the earlier research. In consultation with Dr. Thomas Koerner, vice president/publisher at Rowman & Littlefield, it was decided to build on the earlier work, using it as platform, but to update the policy discussion and the practitioner application. Consequently, two books were written that revisit the earlier work. They can be used as companions or as stand-alones depending on the needs and interests of the reader.

Educators at the Bargaining Table: Successfully Negotiating a Contract That Works for All focuses on preparing for the bargaining table and bargaining the contract at the table. It provides a hands-on full bargaining simulation. *Educators at the Bargaining Table* has a decidedly practical approach to collective bargaining asking what occurs at the bargaining table and what should occur before sitting at the bargaining table. It provides examples and perspectives for consideration by the reader.

The discussion and exploration is informed by the author's experience representing school districts at the bargaining table, two plus decades of teaching negotiations, research on labor relations and collective bargaining, and advising and consulting with both labor and management sides of the table. It is grounded in the realities of the table.

The book begins with an Introduction on the Emerging Challenges of Bargaining. It is then organized into two sections plus appendices. There are four chapters in section I, begins with an Introduction on the emerging challenges of bargaining. It is then (1) Conflict and Cooperation: The Tension in Bargaining (2) The Contract and Preparation for Bargaining, (3) At the Table, and (4) Conclusion: Ready to Bargain.

These chapters provide a background and a preparation for section II, "The Simulation": The Arroyo Wells School District Simulation (chapter 6). This simulation is based on *Labor Relations in Education: Policy, Politics, and Practices*. It is updated with new materials added to the simulation, as well as a reorganization.

This volume provides the reader with practical responses to the challenges of negotiating a CBA. It is written from the perspective of the school board, but its recommendations and examples can also equally apply to those who sit on the union side of the table.

Todd A. DeMitchell
John and H. Irene Peters Professor of Education
Professor, Justice Studies Program
University of New Hampshire
Durham, New Hampshire

Acknowledgments

I wish to acknowledge and thank the many students (MEd, EdS, MPA, JD, and PhD) who took my EDUC 968 Collective Bargaining in Education at the University of New Hampshire, Durham, New Hampshire. Their full participation in the Arroyo Wells School District (AWSD) simulation with its many additional hours of bargaining preparation and the seriousness they brought to the table is noteworthy. Their debriefing sessions helped inform the continued development of the simulation through offering many quality suggestions and good questions about bargaining. I continually learn from these students. They made teaching this course most enjoyable. They have inspired me with their commitment to quality negotiations and maintaining and building quality relationships while sitting at the table.

As always, I gratefully thank Terri, my wife of thirty-five-plus years, for her unconditional support of my professional and my personal life.

Chapter 1

Introduction

The Emerging Challenge

First, [unions] operate as political interest groups, working to obtain benefits from the external environment. And, second, they also function as voluntary organizations that must meet members' demands in the type and level of benefits they obtain and the services they provide. The challenge for unions is to obtain sufficient benefits to maintain their membership, while also operating effectively in a world of political bargaining and compromise.

The roots of public-sector collective bargaining are planted deeply in the soil of legal mechanisms. Wisconsin led the way by passing the first state public-sector collective bargaining law in 1959. This allowed a community of public employees, including teachers, to form a union and to petition the state labor law board to elect an exclusive bargaining representative (a union), which would represent the unit of employees in bargaining collectively with their public employer. Wisconsin started the heyday of public-sector collective bargaining in which the majority of states either required school boards to bargain with the teachers' exclusive representative or permitted local districts to do so.

However, just over a half-century later, the nation once again focused on Wisconsin in February and March 2011, when thousands of workers descended on the state capitol for a different purpose. This time they came not to celebrate their victory of 1959 but to save that victory. Workers, including teachers, arrived, some with children in tow, carrying signs, banging drums, and loudly proclaiming their opposition to pending legislation on collective bargaining and the status of their unions.

As a backdrop to the protest, Democratic senators decamped to another state, denying the Republican governor and the Republican majority in the

Senate the quorum necessary to pass the Wisconsin Budget Repair Act, also known as Act 10. It was later passed.

This act was designed to address the deficit in the state's budget. Wisconsin governor Scott Walker cast the argument as repairing the state's budget and addressing the deficit, while for many the subtext and result was an overt assault on public-sector unions. To meet that budget challenge, Governor Walker's legislation changed the collective bargaining law, even though the union had agreed to the governor's wage and benefits offer, by limiting public-sector bargaining to just wages. Terms and conditions of employment, a staple of bargaining, were removed as a subject of bargaining. It also included a requirement that any raise over the consumer price index must be referred to the voters for a referendum vote.

In addition, the legislation forced the union to hold an election recertification vote every year; it allowed employees who benefit from the collectively bargained contract not to pay a fee for the union's work performed on their behalf; public employers under the bill were restricted from collecting the dues of the union members; and the legislation eliminated all collective bargaining rights for employees in the University of Wisconsin System. DeMitchell and Parker-Magagna characterized the bill as "A Bridge Too Far," a thinly veiled attempt to "break the power of the union."[2] Proponents of the governor's bill characterized the legislation as loosening the stranglehold of unions and protecting the taxpayers' pocketbook from the avarice of the voracious appetite of union bosses. Clearly, public-sector unions in Wisconsin were under siege.

Collective bargaining over wages, benefits, and terms and conditions of employment, the major service provided by unions, was under attack. The unions and many commentators argued that the goal was to break the back of public-sector unions by targeting collective bargaining and starving unions of their revenue. The potential consumers (teachers) of union services judge the value of what is received by the efforts of the union in return for their dues by what is secured through bargaining and other activities that enhance the security of the employee.

Why collective bargaining matters: "Though they have attracted little media or, until recently, scholarly attention, teacher collective bargaining agreements shape nearly everything public schools do."[3] Teachers stand at the crossroads of education. Educational leaders can get little done of any lasting value except through the efforts of teachers. Since collective bargaining affects terms and conditions of employment—the work of teachers—what is bargained and how it is bargained is important. What happens at the bargaining table, how the participants treat each other, has consequences for the present and for the future of the schools and the educators who work in those schools.

THE BOOK

This book looks at what happens at the table and underscores the importance of what occurs there. It provides information for the novice regarding what is collective bargaining and provides recommendations for the experienced negotiator to consider. The exploration of preparing for bargaining at the table concludes with a full simulation that can be bargained as part of a hands-on classroom experience.

Labor relations are a reel of film. One end is blank waiting to be imprinted by the actions of the major players. The other is the history of the working relations of the educators, teachers, and administrators and union and management interactions. Consequently, bargaining is not an unconnected event; it is part of the reel of labor relations. The bargaining of a contract is tied to the past and helps to structure the future. What happens at the table does not occur in a vacuum.

Getting Together[4] and *Getting to Yes*[5] serve as conceptual frameworks for bargaining. Consequently, the focus is not on just getting a contract. The success of bargaining is not predicated upon signing the contract. Success is determined by whether the labor relations, employee-employer relations, are enhanced and improved or at a minimum not harmed. After the parties have gotten to yes on the contract, can they get together as needed partners and collaborators?

Bargaining is not successful if one side or the other is angry at the end of bargaining and has a score to settle in the next round of bargaining. An example is found in Rhode Island in 2017. The teachers in East Greenwich, Rhode Island, voted to approve a contract with the school board. However, immediately following the bilateral approval of the collective bargaining agreement (CBA), the union instituted work-to-rule. A union official stated, "We will teach. We will continue to put East Greenwich students and families first, but we will no longer undertake the many extra activities we have historically done."[6] If you cannot live with the contract, do not sign it. That goes for both sides of the bargaining table.

Fisher and Brown in *Getting Together* write, "If we don't feel positive after the last transaction, we may dread the next and have more difficulty dealing with it."[7] Collective bargaining that does not solve problems, but rather creates or perpetuates problems, cannot be considered successful just because two reluctant or angry parties signed the last page of the contract. DeMitchell and Barton found that, when parties at the table viewed bargaining as solving a problem, the less it was perceived as an obstacle.[8]

The book is organized into two major sections. The first is "Bargaining at the Table." It includes a chapter (chapter 2) on enforcing the contract and the considerations of the conflict of interests and the community of interests inherent in collective bargaining; a discussion of preparation for bargaining (chapter 3); bargaining at the table through good faith (chapter 4); and a concluding discussion of being ready to bargain (chapter 5).

This section covers the practice of negotiating: what goes on before you go to the table, what happens at the table, and what happens after the bargaining ends. It explores the requirement to bargain in "good faith" as a touchstone for finding a community of interests between parties while acknowledging the conflict of interest that is inherent in bargaining.

The second section, "The Simulation," is the application of these chapters by preparing to bargain the AWSD simulation. This is a full simulation in which labor and management through ten hours of expedited bargaining try to reach agreement in a contract. AWSD is a fictional school district with a fictional CBA and two comparator school districts. In addition to the unresolved contract sections, the simulation provides demographics and salary schedules from two comparator school districts.

Letters of interest are provided for the union bargaining team (appendix A) and a letter of interest for the management team (appendix B). These letters guide each team providing markers without stating inflexible positions. The bargaining teams must use these letters of interest as their lodestone. Appendix C is an example of letters that can be sent to the bargaining teams by their constituency to get ready for bargaining.

The book is written to be practical, as well as to provide the necessary academic background for understanding how collective bargaining impacts schools and the profession. The chapters are well footnoted to provide an academic foundation for further research and exploration. The simulation provides a challenge in which those at the table must work to find a tentative agreement (TA). While there are many paths to reaching agreement in which both sides serve their interests, these paths are not always clearly marked. The parties must work hard and work together to find their community of interests.

The simulation has been successfully used through its various iterations over twenty-five years of teaching. Although not every expedited bargaining session resulted in a contract, all parties learned valuable lessons about trying to get to yes while building and maintaining good relations.

NOTES

1. Lorraine M. McDonnell and Anthony Pascal, *Teacher Unions and Educational Reform* (Santa Monica, CA: RAND, 1988, April), vii.
2. Todd A. DeMitchell and Martha Parker-Magna, "'A "Law" Too Far?' The Wisconsin Budget Repair Act: Point." *Education Law Reporter* 275 (2012): 1–15.

3. Frederick M. Hess and Martin R. West, *A Better Bargain: Overhauling Teacher Collective Bargaining for the 21st Century* (Cambridge, MA: Harvard University, Program on Education Policy and Governance, March 29, 2006), 9.

4. Roger Fisher and Scott Brown, *Getting Together: Building Relationships as We Negotiate* (New York: Penguin Books, 1988).

5. Roger Fisher and William Ury, *Getting to Yes: Negotiating Agreement without Giving In* (New York: Penguin Books, 1981).

6. Brenda Lasevoli, "Fed-Up Teachers in R.I. Town Say They Will Teach, But No More 'Extras.'" *Education Week's Blogs, Teacher Beat* (June 22, 2017), Visited July 2, 2017, available at http://blogs.edweek.rg/edweek/teacherbeat/2017/fed-up_teachers_n_ri_town_say.html.

7. Fisher and Brown, *Getting Together*, 8.

8. Todd A. DeMitchell and Richard M. Barton, "Collective Bargaining and Its Impact on Local Educational Reform Efforts." *Educational Policy* 10 (1996): 366–78.

Section I

BARGAINING AT THE TABLE

Chapter 2

Conflict and Cooperation

The Tension in Bargaining

At their worst, unions and school districts are two prisoners manacled together and slugging it out with their free hands. At their most productive, they are self-interested partners in a joint civic venture.[1]

Senator Hillary Rodham Clinton, in a television advertisement in 2007, for her candidacy for the Democratic nominee for president of the United States, advised, "Know when to stand your ground and when to find common ground."[2] She was talking about politics, but she could easily have been discussing collective bargaining.

Collective bargaining and unionization imply that there is a conflict of interest and a community of interest between the two parties, the union (teachers) and management (school district) (see figure 2.1). "In collective bargaining, power is exercised to resolve inherent conflicts of interest," but "compromise and cooperation are necessary."[3] There is a conflict of interest in that the employees through their union pursue their self-interests. Those self-interests include securing the best wage and benefits and the best working conditions for the employee and for the employer receiving the optimal work from the employee to meets goals of providing an effective and efficient educational program. There is a community of interest as well. Both labor and management want to establish a good work place that allows the employee to maximize his or her work.

Teachers' interests may include a high wage, broad benefits, low class-size, control over their instruction, influence over the curriculum, and maximization of their options. An example of the community of interest is found in the establishment of a bargaining unit. Unions represent a unit of members

Conflict of Interests/Community of Interests

Community of Interests

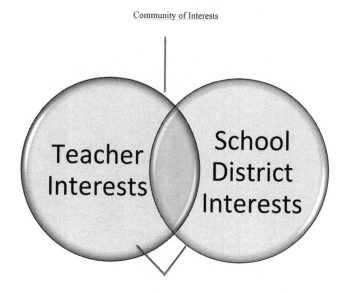

Conflict of Interests

Figure 2.1.   Conditions for Collective Bargaining.

that share similar interests in wages, hours, and working conditions.[4] This allows for an efficiency for bargaining and for contract enforcement. The inclusion of a disparate group of individuals may unnecessarily add complexity to bargaining. This is often highly contested with the union seeking broad inclusion of members and the administration/management seeking a more narrowly defined group of employees to place in the unit.

Management's interests may include providing a reasonable competitive wage, cost-controlled benefits, curriculum alignment through grade levels and subjects and across schools, accountability for student outcomes and providing a cost-effective instructional program. These interests are legitimate and many times in conflict with each other.

Collective bargaining embraces both conflict and community. If there is only conflict, there may be no way to achieve a contract. If there is only a community of interest, is there anything to bargain? Agreement is assured. Both are part of the bargaining process and both are legitimate. If there is no community of interest that can be served through bargaining, there will be nothing but conflict. The tension between conflict and community is inherent and normal. Both are legitimate. How to find the community of interest and

Figure 2.2. Zone of Possible Agreement.

to capitalize on it while simultaneously realizing that conflict is real and will not go away is the challenge of labor relations both at the negotiating table and away from the table.

Another way to conceptualize the community and conflict of interests in bargaining is to review the concept of the zone of possible agreement (ZOPA) (see figure 2.2). While it tends to focus on bargaining over buying and selling, the concept can be applied to education. Essentially, a ZOPA looks for that place in bargaining between two parties where they would walk away from the potential bargain if they do not enter the zone of possible agreement.[5]

This chapter starts with the conflict found in labor relations by reviewing the three major vehicles for addressing conflict, grievances, impasse, and unfair labor practices (ULPs). This section begins with the twin propositions that grievances are our friends and school administrators should wear their small grievance hat when processing grievances. Most of my students are very skeptical about both of these propositions until we talked about what they mean. Hopefully, I have won some converts. The second section will review bargaining concepts that I use in my classes and which form the core of my approach to labor relations, including bargaining.

Conflict is not confined to collective bargaining. It is, in many ways, a constant in social life. School administrators encounter conflict in many different settings apart from the contract. Building conflict resolution skills is a vital skill for leaders, whether they are formal or informal leaders. However, this section is not an exhaustive discussion of the topic of conflict resolution.[6]

CONFLICT OF INTERESTS: LABOR DISPUTES

Clark Kerr considered labor relations to be a form of conflict driven in large part by differences in needs and desires. He characterized this conflict as normal if not necessary. He wrote, "If labor and management are to retain their institutional identities, they must disagree and must act in this disagreement. Conflict is essential to survival."[7] Conflict leads to disputes and because public-sector collective bargaining was instituted to achieve labor peace and harmony in the workplace,[8] consequently, mechanisms were developed to address conflict. Conflict resolution is used when managing the contract (grievances), bargaining the contract (impasse), and labor relations (ULPs).

Grievances: Our Friend and the Grievance Hat

It is important to start with what is a grievance. "The grievance procedure is intended to provide an orderly and fair dispute resolution method."[9] A grievance is an alleged violation, misapplication, or misinterpretation of a specific section of the CBA. It is not a disagreement with any decision that school administrators make. All conflicts are not grievances. Grievances that access the grievance procedures of the contract must be confined to addressing problems arising from the application and/or interpretation of the contract. To use the grievance procedure for any and all disagreements is to expand the contract without the benefit of bargaining. The grievance process was fashioned through the collective bargaining process to address problems associated with conflict regarding the implementation contract.

There is a tendency to believe that grievances are bad things and that they are indicative of administrative failure or employee venality and retaliation. I prefer to approach grievances differently. Grievances can be our friends. They provide a process for defining what the contract means. Sometimes it is a difficult process and one that can be overused and abused, but it is a legitimate conflict resolution procedure. All too often administrators react negatively to grievances with displays of anger, embarrassment, and hurt feelings. While these emotions are real, they have no place within the administration of the contract. The following may be helpful when confronted with a grievance.

- Keep the process professional and keep the responses focused on the alleged violations of the contract. An emotional response to grievances enables the process to be used as a cudgel to keep administrators off balance and under control. Having a grievance filed is neither a badge of distinction nor a badge of shame.
- Understand the grievance using good listening skills. If the grievance is not clear or if it is vague, seek clarity by asking questions. You cannot resolve that which you do not understand.
- Know specifically what section(s) of the contract are alleged to have been violated, misinterpreted, or misapplied. Do not accept general statements. This keeps a focus, so only the problem stated in the grievance is resolved. Do not allow the filing of a grievance to turn into a fishing expedition or a boundary spanning exercise.
- If the grievance does not cite a specific section of the contract, reject the grievance because it is not a grievance. It may be a problem, but it is not a grievance. It may be a problem, but it is not a problem with the contract.

- What is the proposed remedy advanced in the grievance? Is it reasonable? Does it solve the grievance or does it create unintended consequences? Always ask what does this mean in the future if I implement this remedy.
- Consult with other administrators, particularly at the District Office, as to whether there have been similar grievances filed on this section. Consult the grievance log.
- Both the union and management can use grievances to work through differences of opinion and help to resolve conflict or it can be used to heighten conflict. Management cannot control the union's use of the process; it can control its response to the use of the process. This approach does not mean that management cannot respond firmly and clearly when the process is being abused. It does mean that grievances are not the enemy of good leadership. Both parties can explore how the contract is implemented or whether it applies to new and novel situations.
- Grievances should trigger an analysis of the targeted contract section for ambiguity, relevance, and efficiency.
- Good leadership on both sides takes these opportunities to respond to conflict to model professional, honest behavior, to improve relationships, and to move the institution forward. This furthers a community of interest out of a conflict of interest.

Using the description of the small grievance hat provides a vision that grievances are a specific conflict resolution tool. Grievances are not the only strategy; they are, however, the ones that both parties agreed to use in the specific case of conflict involving the contract. It is unwise to use the grievance process to solve conflict that arises outside of the contract. Develop strategies for solving those other conflicts.

Grievances can be our friend when we approach them as opportunities to resolve conflicts and occasions to gain a greater understanding of the contours and conditions of work under a contract. Grievances can remain our friend when they are confined to the job they were created to do applying the contract consistently and fairly. Grievances become unwieldy when they are used to solve all problems and misunderstandings that arise. The grievance process was bargained in good faith; it must be applied in good faith—for that which it was intended to cover.

All conflicts are not grievances. Grievances that access the grievance procedures of the contract must be contained to addressing problems arising from the application or interpretation of the contract. To use the grievance procedure for any and all disagreements is to expand the contract without the benefit of bargaining. This does not mean that the school administrator should disregard a concern about a decision that it is not a grievance; it just means that a separate conflict resolution process must be used. Employees have a right to access appropriate processes to address legitimate concerns. To do less by management is to injure labor relations. The grievance hat is small only allowing the construct to fit under it. Grievances should not be 10 gallon hats in which all difficulties can be addressed.

Arbitration

Many, if not most, contracts have arbitration as part of the grievance process. Arbitration relating to the enforcement of a contract is called rights arbitration. When arbitration is used to settle a contract, it is called interest arbitration. The use of interest arbitration is limited most often to public safety.

Arbitration of a grievance is either advisory or binding. This is a bargainable subject. Advisory arbitration results in a written position delivered by the arbitrator. It is, as its name implies, an advisory opinion; it cannot be imposed on the parties. Binding arbitration is a quasi-judicial opinion; it must be implemented. It is less of a problem-solving character and more of a judicial character.

An arbitrator's task is to interpret the contract and apply it to the dispute/grievance. The U.S. Supreme Court in *United Steelworkers v. Enterprise Wheel & Car Corporation* articulated the standard used in both private-sector and public-sector arbitrations. The Court held:

> An arbitrator is confined to interpretation and application of the collective bargaining agreement; he does not sit to dispense his own brand of industrial justice. He may, of course, look for guidance from many sources, yet his award is legitimate only so long as it draws its essence from the collective bargaining agreement.[10]

Most collective bargaining contracts include language that states that the arbitrator shall have no power to alter, add to, or subtract from the specific language of the contract.[11] In an interesting case out of Indiana, an arbitrator's award was upheld by the state's Court of Appeals. The arbitrator ordered the school district to issue a letter of apology for disciplining a teacher in violation of the CBA.[12] The requirement to apologize is typically not part of a CBA.

Arbitration is similar, but not quite as formal with clearly stated administrative regulations, to a courtroom hearing in which the advocates for both parties extensively prepare, evidence is presented, and witnesses are questioned. Arbitrators use three elements: the language of the contract, the intent of the parties, and past practice,[13] to reach a decision.

While binding arbitration awards require their implementation, the parties to the arbitration can appeal to the courts. One basis, as noted earlier, occurs when the arbitrator's award does not flow from the "essence" of the contract, and the second basis for overturning an arbitrator's decision is a violation of public policy. For example, an arbitrator's award in favor of a seventh-grade math teacher who was facing termination for misconduct involving unwelcome contact with seventh-grade female students including "holding their hands, and/or rubbing their backs or legs."[14] The school district appealed the arbitrator's decision. The Commonwealth Court of Pennsylvania held that the decision, even though it was based on the essence of the contract, violated the well-defined and established public policy that protects students' from sexual harassment by their teachers.[15]

TEXT BOX 2.1

HOW AN ARBITRATOR VIEWS CONTRACT LANGUAGE

1. What was the intent of the parties?
   - How is this substantiated: recall of oral conversation; implied intent, or written record of intent?
   - The minutes of the negotiating sessions can be very valuable.
2. Who proposed the language?
   - Generally, the party who proposed the language bears the responsibility of proving its intent.
3. If the language is clear and unambiguous, an arbitrator need only look at the "four corners" of the agreement.
4. What was the past practice of the parties regarding the disputed section if the language is ambiguous or silent?
5. What objections and concessions were made during the course of bargaining the disputed section?
6. The words of the contract language are given their ordinary meaning: the "plain meaning rule."
7. The language is read in its entirety, not just one specific passage.
8. Specific language controls general language.
9. Absurd results must be avoided.
10. The arbitrator uses the concept of "reasonableness." What is reasonable under the circumstances?

School districts that argue against binding arbitration assert that the school board is the elected body and that it should not give up its decision-making authority to an outside party. While the argument makes a good political statement, it may not have the force of law. Many state public employment boards, similar to the National Labor Relations Board (NLRB),[16] have held that a workable grievance procedure must end with some form of binding arbitration from an outside party. If the contract does not have a "workable" grievance procedure, the grievance may be elevated to an ULP. Thus, a third party makes a binding decision anyway, destroying the argument for not negotiating binding arbitration. The U.S. Supreme Court in *Moses H. Cone v. Hospital v. Mercury Construction Corporation* (1983) stated a preference for arbitration over litigation.[17]

An advantage in bargaining binding arbitration is that it provides an opportunity to clearly state if there are sections of the contract that are not appropriate to take to arbitration. This is called positive assurance. All sections of a contract are considered open to the grievance process if there is an arbitration clause. The concept was articulated in *United Steelworkers of America v. Warrior & Gulf Navigation Company*. The U.S. Supreme Court opined that there is a presumption of arbitrability of a grievance "unless it can be said with positive assurance that the arbitration clause is not susceptible of an interpretation that covers the dispute."[18] Various state employment boards and courts have applied this concept to public-sector bargaining.[19]

If a section of the contract, such as the content of an evaluation or observation, is considered inappropriate for third-party arbitration, then that section can be bracketed with a statement that it is not subject to either the grievance process or arbitration. Positive assurance is then gained because both parties have agreed to clear, unambiguous language through a meeting of the minds at the bargaining table.

Impasse

Impasse is another conflict resolution process. It is used when negotiations on the contract have stalled to the point that no further progress is being made and is not likely to be made. Impasse should only be declared when no movement is being made on any of the sections of the contract and further bargaining would be futile. As long as a single issue is being negotiated with some success—ongoing discussion and/or trading proposals—impasse should not be declared. In a NLRB decision, the board held that both parties must believe that they are at the "end of their rope."[20] The process for declaring impasse and instituting the impasse procedures vary by states.

Impasse typically involves two actions, mediation followed by fact-finding. Mediation involves a third-party mediator meeting with the two parties separately and at times together. The goal of the mediator is to get an agreement. The goal is not to fashion a wise agreement; it is to get agreement. One state mediator working with a school district and a union representing teacher aides summed it up this way, "Tell me what it will take to wrap it up."[21] Deborah Kolb, in her research on mediators, characterized state mediators, the ones who mediate public-sector collective bargaining, as deal makers. For example, in her analysis she quotes a mediator, "I come in, I want to make a deal. I need something to work with."[22]

If mediation is not successful, the parties go to fact-finding. Fact-finding is advisory. The goal is for each party to present their best argument for their position using facts to support their position. The fact finder analyzes the position of both parties and renders a decision as to which positions are supported by the facts. This decision is typically advisory, which reduces the effectiveness and efficiency of fact-finding as a conflict resolution strategy.

The last labor dispute mechanism is an ULP. Whereas, a grievance is an allegation of a violation of the contract, an ULP is allegation of a violation of the state public-sector collective bargaining law. ULPs are state-specific, with each state defining what constitutes an ULP. A violation of good faith bargaining by making a unilateral change in wages, benefits, or terms and conditions of employment is a common ULP. Another is management interfering with the union's right of exclusive representation through management by either offering inducements or threats through direct dealing.

ULPs can be filed by the union against management/employer or by the employer against the union. The latter are the most common petitioner with less ULPs being filed by management. A third option is for an employee to file a grievance against the union. When this happens, it is typically an allegation of the failure of the duty of fair representation.

For example, in New York, a teacher filed an ULP, in part, against his union alleging a violation of the duty of fair representation when the union decided not to pursue one of his grievances.[23] Unions are not required to pursue all grievances to arbitration.

PAST PRACTICE

Another area that often is the focus of conflict resulting in grievances, arbitration, and ULPs is past practice. Both sides assert it when they believe that it serves their interests with both sides providing either an expansive or a minimal definition of what constitutes a past practice. But what is it?

Past practice is an often-stated concept, but most often it is little understood. Arbitrator Richard Mittenthal's definition of past practice is widely accepted. He defines a past practice as "a course of conduct that is the understood and accepted way of doing things over an extended period of time, and thus mutually binding and enforceable."[24] A past practice becomes important when the contract is silent or ambiguous on a particular practice. Consequently, a past practice is typically not written down. The key is that the past practice must be a consistent and clear practice and not an isolated event. It must have occurred over a period of time. It must be known and accepted by both parties. The party asserting a past practice typically carries the burden of demonstrating that the practice has existed and under what conditions it has occurred.

The Supreme Court of New Hampshire provides some useful guidance in this area. In an appeal from a New Hampshire Public Employee Labor Relations Board (PELRB) decision (2007-026), the Tamworth Educational Support Personnel Association alleged that the school district had agreed to a just cause provision through past practice and statements made in the collective bargaining negotiations. There was no specific provision for just cause bargained into the contract language. On the issue of what constitutes a past practice, the Court wrote (some internal citations omitted):

> Under certain circumstances, custom and past practice may establish an implied term of a collective bargaining agreement. In the *Appeal of New Hampshire Department of Safety*, for instance the evidence established that the past practice at issue existed "over the course of the employment relationship" between the union and the employer. The practice continued openly, was never modified by multiple collective bargaining agreements into which the parties entered, and inexorably led the PELRB to conclude that "both parties had knowledge that the past practice existed and by their respective actions over the protracted period of time demonstrated acceptance of it." By contrast, the evidence [in the *Appeal of Tamworth*] concerned a single employee's experience in July 2005. The PELRB reasonably determined that this offer of proof was insufficient to establish a binding past practice.[25]

Similarly, David Cohen, writing for *Labor Notes*, posits the following test for establishing a past practice. The practice:

- has existed for a reasonably long time;
- occurs repeatedly;
- is clear and consistent;
- must be known to both management and union;
- must be accepted by both management and union;[26] and
- is not contrary to clear and unambiguous language in the CBA.[27]

Even with these guidelines a question that often surfaces is what if there is clear language in the contract that management has not uniformly enforced, such as teachers must submit lesson plans on Fridays at 3:30 p.m. If management has not consistently enforced this provision, has a past practice been established that precludes the enforcement of the clearly stated contract provision? Generally, the answer is no. If there is a bargained right, the party who bargained the right is entitled to enforce the clear language. The party does not need to wait until the contract expires to start exercising the right.[28]

However, it is a good practice to talk with the union or with management to give them a heads-up about your decision to start enforcing the clear contract provision. It is an opportunity to "discuss, listen, consider and then go ahead with your plan if you still believe it makes sense."[29] It is not seeking permission to enforce the contract.

BUILDING A COMMUNITY OF INTEREST

As stated earlier, bargaining has a tension between conflict of interests and a community of interests. The conflict will not go away. There is, however, an inherent community of interest founded on the professional service rendered by educators through the organization of a school. A challenge is how to maintain and expand that community of interest within the confines of the conflict of interests There is no silver bullet and no magic incantation that makes bargaining easy, turning it into a "Kumbaya moment." It is hard work, but anchoring bargaining and labor relations with concepts and approaches helps.

We are all negotiators; whether or not we sit at a formal table with two sides, we negotiate many things in our life. It is one of the basic ways by which one individual gets something from another. An Italian diplomat, Daniel Vare, once said that negotiation is the "art of letting them have your way."[30] "It is a back-and-forth communication designed to reach agreement when you and the other side have some interests that are shared and others that are opposed."[31] Negotiations are predicated on getting the other side to say yes to what you want. Individuals negotiate because they believe that they can get something that could not be had without negotiations.

The following will discuss two well-known and respected books that set the stage for negotiating at the table or away from the table.

Getting to Yes

Roger Fisher and William Ury, as part of the Harvard Negotiations Project, developed the concept of "principled negotiations." The four basic points of principled negotiations are as follows:

1. People: Separate the people from the problem;
2. Interests: Focus on interests, not positions;
3. Options: Generate a variety of possibilities before deciding what to do; and
4. Criteria: Insist that the result be based on some objective standard.[32]

These four aspects of principled negotiations can produce a wise agreement through fair negotiations. A wise agreement should be efficient and should improve or at least not damage the relationship between parties. As stated in the Introduction chapter, it is the relationship between the parties that will carry on long after the ink from the signatures has dried. The relationship will be the indicator of the success of negotiations. Signing a contract is not the measure of success of negotiations; success is measured by how the parties treat each other afterwards, has their relationship improved and can the new contract be implemented and managed by fairness and trust or will suspicion and the need to get even define the relationship? Embattled and embittered teachers and administrators signal a continuation of hostilities following the brief lull after signing the contract. Battle lines for the next round of negotiations get drawn early.

Fisher's and Ury's first rule of negotiating is, "Don't bargain over positions." There is comfort in having and holding a position. The anchor of a position, however, tends to keep you in one place when options and possibilities best serve the interests you are pursuing at the table. Protecting positions often produces unwise and inefficient agreements. Bargaining over positions often results in the negotiator identifying worth as a negotiator with securing her/his party's position and denying the position of the other party. Too often "positional bargaining becomes a contest of wills"[33] with the requisite winner and loser.

Instead of adopting a position and bargaining to secure that position, Fisher and Ury suggest that you focus on your interests and not on your position. The following are some of the suggestions to advance your interests at the table:

- Talk about your interests. One of the purposes of negotiating is to serve your interests.
- Be hard on the problem but soft on the people. You are trying to resolve the problem not harm individuals or the relationship. "If negotiators view themselves as adversaries in a personal face-to-face confrontation, it is difficult to separate their relationship from the substantive problem."[34]
- Put the problem before your answer. Give your interests and reasoning first and your conclusions or proposals later.
- "You will satisfy your interests better if you talk about where you would like to go rather than about where you have come from."[35]

If the other side wants to engage in positional bargaining, they suggest trying the following:

- When the other side sets forth their position, neither reject it nor accept it. Look for their interest that lies behind it. What are they seeking from this language?

- Treat their proposal as one possible solution. This is consistent with good faith bargaining.
- Instead of asking the other side to accept or reject your ideas, ask them what is wrong with the idea.
- Ask questions and then remember to pause giving them time to generate answers. Silence is too little used; often silence makes individuals uncomfortable and they seek to fill the silence. Also, it is important to remember that when your mouth is closed as you listen, it is hard to fit your foot into it.[36]
- Question their tactics, not their personal integrity.
- Do not undermine your credibility by making extreme demands that both parties know will be abandoned. In other words, do not squander credibility; it is hard to get and even harder to maintain.
- Yield to reason, not pressure.

Just being nice (Cannot we just get along?), however, is not the answer. A hard game dominates a soft game. This does not mean that you should yield to pressure or let yourself be coerced; yield only to principle and reason, not pressure. The outcome of principled negotiations should improve relations but focusing on the relationship to the exclusion of furthering your interests runs the risk of attaining neither. The hard game should focus on the problem and not on the people. A wise agreement is not reached by giving in; too often it feeds the appetite from the other side to gain more by pressuring more. Do not allow it to become effective.

A strategy that Fisher and Ury suggest is developing a best alternative to a negotiated agreement (BATNA). They assert that it "will protect you against both accepting an agreement you should reject and rejecting an agreement you should accept."[37] A BATNA provides a standard by which negotiations can be measured in satisfying management or the union's interests.

Maurer asserts that a BATNA removes mental pressure to reach an agreement and it gives a criterion for measuring proposals.[38] Fisher and Ury believe that in most circumstances the greater danger is being too committed to reaching an agreement and being unduly pessimistic about negotiations being broken off. A well-developed BATNA increases the ability to improve the terms of any negotiated agreement.

Getting Together

The sequel to *Getting to Yes* is *Getting Together*.[39] This book takes the basic ideas about negotiation (stated earlier) and focuses on the relationship of shared and conflicting interests. It is notable that Fisher branches out from the first book by choosing to explore in greater detail the relationship that exists between the parties. The overall theme of the book is the importance of pursuing a "working relationship," one that can deal with the inherent differences of a relationship.

In many ways, *Getting Together* may be the beginning point. Collective bargaining in education involves negotiations between two parties who know each other. They come to the table with a relationship and will have a relationship once they leave the table. If the relationship is poor before bargaining begins, there is diminished hope that acrimony will dry up and wither away on its own. In contrast, a strong relationship smoothes the path for mutual gain. An improved labor relationship is one of the themes of this book.

Getting to Yes developed principled negotiations; *Getting Together* advances an unconditionally constructive strategy. This strategy is designed to improve relationships without harming substantive interests pursued at the bargaining table. Their guidelines are not directed on how to be good, but rather on how to be effective. "They derive from a selfish hard-headed concern with what each of us can do, in practical terms, to make a relationship work better."[40] In a nutshell, an unconditionally constructive strategy states, "Do only those things that are good for the relationship and good for us, whether or not they are reciprocated."[41]

The unconditionally constructive strategy seeks a good substantive outcome for both parties, inner peace ("We want to be able to say: 'I can work things out with these people.' "),[42] and an ability to deal with differences. As discussed earlier, collective bargaining takes place in an environment with a community of interests and a conflict of interests. Differences and conflict in relationships are normal; their appearance does not signify that the relationship is in crisis.

The major themes of Fisher's and Brown's strategy are summarized below:

1. Balance reason and emotion: "We need both reason informed by emotion and emotion guided by and tempered by reason."[43] We often act emotionally rather than logically. Emotions are a necessary part of us; we do not choose our emotions, they just happen. Too much emotion can cloud judgment and overwhelm reason and too little can impair motivation and judgment. Parties at the bargaining table should neither press their emotions nor ignore them. They write, "I should no more ignore them than I should ignore any other important fact in negotiation. But my emotional state may cause me to make poor judgments about what to say and what to do."[44]

2. Understanding: Seek to learn how the other side see things. Whether or not the parties agree is not the major point, rather trying to understand each other's perceptions, values, and interests is the major point. One party does not have to accept the other's perception, values, and interests but understanding them allows for a greater chance of finding a community of interest for them.

3. Good communication: Always consult before deciding. Fisher and Brown identify three barriers to effective communication: we assume that there is no need to talk; we communicate in one direction by telling; and we send mixed messages.[45] Good communication facilitates any relationship; poor communication harms all relationships. Developing a habit of communicating is important. They advise both parties at the bargaining table to "inquire, consult, and listen. We both participate in making decisions."[46] Adopting a strategy of no surprises can be helpful. No surprises means communicating early so as to not surprise the other party, possibly forcing them into defensiveness and a feeling of being disregarded.

4. Reliability: Both parties work on being trustworthy. Communication is a wasted opportunity if it is not believed. They pose the following questions: Is our conduct erratic? Do we communicate carelessly? Do we treat even clear promises lightly? And, are we deceptive or dishonest?"[47] Be wholly trustworthy but not wholly trusting.

5. Persuasion, not coercion, is most helpful: As stated in *Getting to Yes*, one should not give into coercion. The less likely, according to the authors, that the outcome will reflect the concerns of both parties, the less likely it will be accepted. Coercion tends to damage the quality of an agreement: a coerced agreement may not have been crafted to meet the interests of both parties; it may not benefit from creative thinking, and its legitimacy as measured by standards of fairness is questioned. Individuals do not like to feel that they are being coerced. If it does not work against me, why would it work for me?

6. Mutual acceptance: It acknowledges the long-term relationship. Acceptance does not mean approval; it means accepting the other parties' right to have views that differ. Good relations are not easy to achieve; they involve hard work. However, giving in to appease does not work. "It may avoid arguments, but it also eliminates the opportunity to learn how to talk through problems and to become skillful at reaching solutions."[48]

TEXT BOX 2.2

ACHIEVING EFFECTIVE WORKING RELATIONSHIPS

To achieve our substantive goals, we need effective working relationships, relationships that have a high degree of rationality, understanding, communication, reliability, noncoercive means of influence, and acceptance.

Source: Roger Fisher & Scott Brown, Getting Together: Building Relationships as We Negotiate (New York: Penguin Books, 1988): 14–15.

If labor and management treat each other with respect and pay attention to the process of collective bargaining, then it may be easier to successfully negotiate a contract that works for both parties. *Getting to Yes* and *Getting Together* may help to build on the community of interest that exists in our schools, while not negating the conflict of interest that exists. Fisher and Brown conclude:

> Discussing honestly our joint ability to deal with differences is almost certain to reduce misunderstandings, improve communication, and convey the message that each of the parties accepts the other as someone with a contribution to make in dealing with joint problems. A good working relationship will work even better when we work on it together.[49]

How we respond to the other side is within our control. We cannot control the other, we can only control ourselves and how we respond. Do we seek to expand the community of interest or contract it? Do we seek to emphasize differences and embrace our conflicts? Each party decides how to answer these questions. "It would be a mistake to define a good relationship as one in which we agree easily, just as it would be a mistake to define a good road as one that is easy to build."[50]

A last consideration of a community of interest is win-win bargaining which seeks to emphasise the community of interest. This begs the question of whether there has to be losers when bargaining. While there are many forms of win-win bargaining, this brief discussion will look at one representative author, William Keane, as an example. Keane writes, "The basic premise of bargaining in a win/win mode is the assumption that both parties see the best interests of their constituents most efficiently served by helping the other party meet the interests of its own constituents simultaneously."[51] He offers five principles for those who pursue win-win bargaining.

1. Facilitate the growth of trust; do not demand it.
2. Separate resource-allocation issues from problem-resolution issues.
3. Start by exchanging problems, not solutions.

   Presentation of problems

   A This is our problem.
   B These are the reasons that this issue is a problem for us.
   C Here are the facts that demonstrate that this is a problem.[52]

4. Brainstorm solutions for problems.
5. Freely share relevant information.

Some common points of win-win bargaining include, frequent year-round meetings to discuss problems as they come up rather than waiting for the contract to expire, keeping communications open, helping each other win, using a problem-solving approach rather than trying to win points, and developing a trusting relationship. Some have recommended that outside negotiators not be used, arguing that the people at the table must have stake in the outcome and in the relationship. Trust and reliability are critical traits to build and maintain. There does not appear to be any magic about win-win bargaining. The approach to win-win makes sense whether it is called win-win or just plain old-fashioned bargaining that wants to get the job done. What may set it apart is the conscious decision that both parties want to do something different and commit to making a difference at the bargaining table and away from the bargaining table. It acknowledges the conflict of interest and focuses on building and emphasizing the community of interest.

At the end of the day of bargaining, there is no magic formula or perfect process that moves everyone to win-win bargain resulting in the "Elegant Solution" (see chapter 4). It is hard work that does not end. The garden must always be tended, lest it be overgrown with weeds and revert back to its original wild state. If there is any magic in the process, it is in the individuals who remain committed to doing it differently and trying to do it better. Individuals who are committed to improving the relationship make the difference.

NOTES

1. Charles Taylor Kerchner and Krista D. Caufman, "Building the Airplane While It's Rolling down the Runway." In Charles Taylor Kerchner and Julia E. Koppich, *A Union of Professionals: Labor Relations and Educational Reform* (New York: Teachers College Press, 1993), 1–24, 2.

2. Senator Hillary Rodham Clinton (December 17, 2007), WMUR Channel 9 (ABC affiliate).

3. Anthony M. Cresswell and Michael J. Murphy, with Charles T. Kerchner, *Teachers, Unions, and Collective Bargaining in Public Education* (Berkeley, CA: McCutchan Publishing Corporation, 1980), 191.

4. 29 U.S.C. § 159(c)(5) (1952).

5. Brad Spangler, "Zone of Possible Agreement (ZOPA)." In Guy Burgess and Heidi Burgess (eds.), *Beyond Intractability*. Conflict Information Consortium, University of Colorado, Boulder. Visited January 23, 2014, available at http://www.beyondintractability.org/essay/zopa. I wish to acknowledge and thank Dr. Martha Parker Magnana for introducing me to this concept and for guest lecturing in my labor relations class.

6. For an expanded discussion of conflict resolution within a bargaining environment, I suggest the following:

- Max Bazermann and Margaret Neale, *Negotiating Rationally* (Cambridge, MA: Harvard University Press, 2006).

- Robert H. Mnookin, Scott R. Peppet, and Andrew S. Tulumello, *Beyond Winning: Negotiating to Create Value in Deals and Disputes* (Cambridge, MA: The Belknap Press of Harvard University, 2004).
- Douglas Stone, Bruce Patton, and Sheila Heen, *Difficult Conversations: How to Discuss What Matters* (New York: Viking, 1999).

7. Clark Kerr, "The Nature of Industrial Conflict." In E. Wight Bakke, Clark Kerr, and Charles W. Anrod (eds.), *Unions, Management, and the Public* (San Diego, CA: Harcourt Brace Jovanovich, 1967), 246.

8. In New Hampshire, public sector collective bargaining was developed to "foster harmonious and cooperative relations between public employers and their employees to protect the public by encouraging the orderly and uninterrupted operation of government." Chapter 490, December 21, 1975. Statement of Policy New Hampshire Revised Statutes Annotated § 273-A. Visited January 17, 2009, available at http://www.nh.gov/pelrb/. In Illinois, "the Illinois General Assembly declared the purpose of the IELRA was to promote orderly and constructive relationships between educational employees and their employers, recognizing that harmonious relationships are required between educational employees and their employers." Visited January 17, 2009, available at http://www.illinois.gov/elrb/.

9. John W. Budd, *Labor Relations: Striking a Balance* (Boston, MA: McGraw-Hill Irwin, 2005), 332.

10. *United Steelworkers v. Enterprise Wheel & Car Corporation*, 363 U.S. 593, 596 (1960).

11. However, in *Marion Community School Corporation v. Marion Teachers Association*, 873 N.E.2d 605 (Ind. App. 2007), the Indiana Court of Appeals upheld an arbitrator's award for attorney's fees for the prevailing union even though there was no provision for attorney's fees in the contract. In addition, the arbitrator's requirement that the school district issue an apology to the grievant in an effort to make the grievant whole for potential loss to his reputation was upheld. The Court writes, "An apology teaches the School Corporation to follow the Agreement in the future and also not to make derogatory comments in the newspaper. Indiana law provides an arbitrator with the broad remedial authority to make such an award." P. 610.

12. *Marion Community School Corporation v. Marion Teachers Association*, 873 N.E.2d 605 (Ind. App. 2007).

13. For example, the City of Oswego, New York, violated past practice when it unilaterally prohibited firefighters from washing and waxing their private vehicles in the city fire stations during work time. The New York Public Employment Relations Board found that the Fire Chief's awareness and acceptance/acquiescence of the practice established a past practice that required bargaining if a change in the practice is sought. *City of Oswego Firefighters Association, IAFF, Local 2701 and City of Oswego*, U-27221, May 20, 2008.

14. *Bethel Park School v. Bethel Park Federation*, 55 A.2d 154, 155–56 (Pa. Commonwealth 2012).

15. Ibid., 162.

16. *See Collier Insulated Wire*, 192 N.L.R.B. 837 (1971).

17. *Moses H. Cone Hospital v. Mercury Construction Corporation*, 460 U.S. 1, 25 (1983) (writing "Congress declared a national policy favoring arbitration and withdrew the power of states to require a judicial forum for the resolution of claims which the contracting parties agreed to resolve by arbitration"). *See*, for an opposing view, Jean R. Sternlight, "Panacea or Corporate Tool: Debunking the Supreme Court's Preference for Binding Arbitration" 74 *Washington University Law Quarterly* 637, 711 (1996) (concluding, "The Court should abandon its unjustified preference for arbitration and replace it with a policy of acceptance of arbitration voluntarily agreed to by contracting parties").

18. *United Steelworkers of America v. Warrior & Gulf Navigation Company*, 363 U.S. 574, 582–83 (1960).

19. See *New Britain Board of Education v. New Britain Federation of Teachers, Local 871*, 754 F. Supp.2d 407 (D. Conn. 2010); *Appeal of Londonderry School District*, 142 N.H. 677, 680, 707 A.2d 137, 139 (1998) (writing, "[1] Arbitration is a matter of contract and a party cannot be required to submit to arbitration any dispute which he has not agreed so to submit.; [2] unless the parties clearly state otherwise, the question of whether the parties agreed to arbitrate is to be decided by the court, not the arbitrator; [3] a court should not rule on the merits of the parties' underlying claims when deciding whether they agreed to arbitrate; and [4] under the 'positive assurance' standard, when a CBA contains an arbitration clause, a presumption of arbitrability exists, and in the absence of any express provision excluding a particular grievance from arbitration, . . . only the most forceful evidence of a purpose to exclude the claim from arbitration can prevail").

20. *A.M.F. Bowling Company*, 314 N.L.R.B. 969 (1994).

21. Deborah M. Kolb, *The Mediators* (Cambridge, MA: MIT Press, 1983), 27.

22. Ibid. See pages 23–28, for an interesting discussion of a mediator as a dealmaker.

23. *Antonio Jenkins and United Federation of Teachers, Local 2, AFT, AFL-CIO and Board of Education of the City School District of the City of New York*, U-26822, April 3, 2008.

24. Richard Mittenthal, "Past Practice and Administration of Collective Bargaining Agreements" *Michigan Law Review* 59, no. 7 (1961).

25. *Appeal of Tamworth Educational Support Personnel Association*, Case No. 2007–0339, (March 24, 2008) *slip opinion*.

26. David Cohen (December 22, 2008), "Understanding and Defending Past Practices." *Labor Notes*. Visited July 31, 2017, available at http://www.labornotes. org/2008/12/understanding-and-defending-past-practices.

27. P. A. Flaherty-Hood (February 11, 2011). "Employment Past Practices: Binding or Not?" Visited July 31, 2017, available at http://www.flaherty-hood.com/ employment-practices-binding-not/.

28. Thomas C. Pence (May 16, 2016), "Changing Past Practices—You Might Already Have the Right to Do What You Want." *Labor & Employment Law Perspectives*. Visited July 31, 2017, available at https://www.laboremploymentperspectives.com/2016/05/16/ changing-past-practices-you-might-already-have-the-right-to-do-what-you-want/.

29. Ibid.

30. David A. Lax and James K. Sebenius, *3D Negotiations: Powerful Tools to Change the Game in Your Most Important Deals* (Cambridge, MA: Harvard Business School Press, 2006), 37.

31. Roger Fisher and William Ury, *Getting to Yes: Negotiating Agreement without Giving In* (New York: Penguin Books, 1981), xi.

32. Ibid., 10.

33. Ibid., 6.

34. Ibid., 38.

35. Ibid., 54.

36. "If they have made an unreasonable proposal or attack you regard as unjustified, the best thing to do may be to sit there and not say a word." Ibid., 117.

37. Ibid., 104.

38. Richard E. Maurer, *Managing Conflict: Tactics for School Administrators* (Boston, MA: Allyn and Bacon, 1991), 113.

39. Roger Fisher and Scott Brown, *Getting Together: Building Relationships as We Negotiate* (New York: Penguin Books, 1988).

40. Ibid., 38.

41. Ibid. "The high moral content of the guidelines is a bonus."

42. Ibid., 8.

43. Ibid., 10.

44. Ibid., 54.

45. Ibid., 86.

46. Ibid., 40.

47. Ibid., 109–11.

48. Ibid., 21.

49. Ibid., 192.

50. Ibid., 5.

51. William G. Keane, *Win Win or Else: Collective Bargaining in an Age of Public Discontent* (Thousand Oaks, CA: Corwin Press, Inc., 1996), 36.

52. Ibid., 32.

Chapter 3

The Contract and Preparation for Bargaining

Though they have attracted little media or, until recently, scholarly attention, teacher collective bargaining agreements shape nearly everything public schools do.[1]

Often we prepare for bargaining by thinking about where we want to begin. Good negotiations begin by thinking about where we would like to end. This understanding enables the bargain team to chart our path for getting there.[2]

The mantra for bargaining is prepare, prepare, prepare. This is a lesson that is often learned early, but earned the hard way by not being prepared. Fisher and Ertel assert that in negotiations "the lack of preparation is perhaps our most serious handicap."[3] Negotiations require data.

Much of the necessary data cannot wait to be gathered until just before starting bargaining. Seniority lists, age of teachers for retirement purposes, history of comparator school district salary raises, fringe benefit costs, five-year comparison costs for early retirement packages, and grievance history are all data sources that the director of labor relations should consistently collect. We will explore what data should be gathered and ways for displaying the data. But, first we will explore what is a contract.

TEXT BOX 3.1

WHAT IS A COLLECTIVE BARGAINING AGREEMENT?

A CBA is a contractual agreement between an employer and a labor union that governs wages, hours, and working conditions for employees

---

and which can be enforced against the employer and the union for failure to comply with its terms.

Source: The Free Dictionary, "Collective Bargaining Agreement." Visited June 24, 2017, available at http://legal-dictionary.thefreedictionary.com/Collective+Bargaining+Agreement.

First, why does a CBA matter? "Though they have attracted little media or, until recently, scholarly attention, teacher collective bargaining agreements shape nearly everything public schools do."[4] Teachers stand at the crossroads of education. Educational leaders can get nothing done of any lasting value for students except through the efforts of teachers working with their students.

Since collective bargaining affects terms and conditions of employment—the work of teachers—what is bargained and how it is bargained is important. Bargaining at its best "is a legitimate vehicle for problem solving."[5] While it has the ability to set parties against each other when there is a conflict of interests, it also has the ability to bring parties together for meaningful discussions in a community of shared interests.

For example, a study of superintendent responses to the impact of collective bargaining on implementing school reform drew mixed comments. A superintendent from a large school district in the South wrote, "The union's actions constrained the school improvement process."[6] However, a rural superintendent stated that bargaining "caused both sides to truly and deeply discuss philosophy."

Either way—positive or negative—bargaining is a process that affects schools. What happens at the table does not stay at the table; the process and outcome ripples outward.

Collective bargaining is the major work of unions; it is what they do. It clearly is the most visible work of unions in school districts. "In collective bargaining, the union is usually the driving force, and its performance in this mode is ordinarily the crucial test of its value to the employees it represents."[7]

A union's stance on policy issues in the political arena may garner the attention of the media and the public, but the work of unions from its members' perspective is bargaining, implementing, and enforcing a contract. The union is judged by how well it does its work for its members. Do the teachers "get" things they would not get except for the support of the union?

MANDATORY, PERMISSIVE, AND PROHIBITED CATEGORIES OF BARGAINING

Collective bargaining moved three critical decisions from the unilateral decision-making of school boards to bilateral decision-making. Prior to unions gaining the right to bargain as the exclusive representative of its members, the employer could make unilateral decisions regarding employment. With collective bargaining, decisions affecting the wages, benefits, and terms and conditions of employment must be bargained.

Employment is classified into three categories for bargaining purposes, mandatory, permissive, and prohibited subjects of bargaining. *Mandatory subjects* must be bargained. They are the core of the CBA and refusal to bargain these subjects is considered a failure to bargain in good faith (see chapter 4, for a discussion of good faith). For example, the number of instructional periods that a teacher must teach each day is a term and condition of employment, which must be bargained.[8]

Another category of bargainable items is *permissive subjects* of bargaining. States regulate the labor contract and labor relations through legislation "but leave the remainder of the teacher's labor contract unspecified."[9] It is this unspecified portion that often forms the subjects that are permissive. While the failure to bargain over a mandatory subject of bargaining gives rise to a legal proceeding called an ULP, neither a school district nor a union are required to bargain over a permissive subject of bargaining.

A permissive subject of bargaining may be raised at the table by one of the parties, typically the union, but the other party can decide that it does want to include the subject in the contract. Neither party "can insist upon such subjects as a condition of executing a contract."[10] In other words, a party cannot insist to impasse that the other party agree on the permissive subject of bargaining.[11] If a party does not want to bargain a subject that is permissible, the party need only say no. It is wise, however, to provide a rationale for the "no" so as to keep getting to yes.

These topics may vary from state to state. For example, in some states class size is considered a permissive subject of bargaining. A school district that decides to bargain a permissive subject of bargaining must approach this decision with caution. Once the subject is in the contract, it will remain in the contract until it is bargained out of the contract.

The third type of bargaining is prohibited. *Prohibited subjects* of bargaining cannot be bargained.

Prohibiting the bargaining of policy keeps policy-making an essential public responsibility that cannot be bargained away. School boards are elected by the public and are responsible to the public via the ballot box. Giving unions the ability to bargain policy removes the public from the policy-making process because unions are not directly accountable to the public.

The Supreme Court of New Jersey in *Ridgefield Park Education Association v. Ridgefield Park Board of Education* buttressed this idea of union separation from public policy formation when it wrote: "The very foundation of representative democracy would be endangered if decisions of significant matters of governmental policy were left to the process of collective negotiations, where citizen participation is precluded."[12] Since policy initiatives are placed by law in the hands of management, the faculty role is often reduced to reaction and response to policy in a collective bargaining environment.

An example of prohibited subjects of bargaining is found in an early public-sector bargaining case, *Aberdeen Education Association v. Aberdeen Board of Education* (1974). The court held that bargaining over teacher use of instructional aides, preparation periods, and teacher conferences should not interfere with the discretion of the elected representatives.[13] Under federal law, proposals that directly implicate other bargaining units is nonnegotiable.[14]

However, while policy is a prohibited subject of bargaining, the impact, or effects, of the policy decision is often considered an appropriate if not a required subject of bargaining. For example, a school district can decide to layoff employees as part of its managerial prerogative. However, because the decision impacts the wages, benefits, and terms and conditions of employment, the school district must bargain the impact of the decision, not the decision itself, if the union demands it.[15]

THE CBA

A challenge that large school districts face in bargaining contracts is the number of contracts that must be bargained. Even though we have focused on bargaining with teacher unions, there are a number of additional unions representing different groups of employees with which a school district may have to bargain.

These differing employee groups have different needs and interests from teachers. However, the school district must attend to these unions and their employee interests with the same care as they do with all other employee groups.

The potential reach of employee groups can be quite large. For example, the Seattle Public Schools bargain one contract with principals, three with the Seattle Education Association, four with the International Union of Operating Engineers, one with the Seattle/King County Building Construction Trades, two with the International Association of Machinists, two with the Teamsters, and one with Pacific Northwest Regional Council of Carpenters.[16]

The more CBAs that need to be bargained, the greater is the complexity of bargaining for management. If management bargains with one union, the others watch closely. If a concession is won by the union bargaining, the others may raise the cry of "me too" so that they can benefit from the work of the other union without trade-offs.

Another important question for this chapter is what is a CBA. Essentially a CBA operates like a contract. It is an agreement between two parties, the union and the school district

- that is enforceable through procedures contained in the contract (grievances, mediation, and arbitration)
- and by external, third party, state administrative agencies (ULPs) similar to the federal NLRB and by the judicial system. Alleged violations of the contract/CBA are not pursued by the usual means of breach of contract.

A CBA has the basic elements of a contract in which both parties agree to the terms and conditions of employment, the wages, and benefits exchanged for the services, which is reduced to writing. However, the CBA is not an individual contract for employment; the school board offers employment contracts. The employees' exclusive representative with the employing school district bargains the CBA on their behalf. Consequently, the employees/members of the bargaining unit must follow the contract.

Table 3.1 depicts many of the common characteristics of a teacher CBA.

In order to properly prepare for bargaining, negotiator must gather and analyze data. Listed below are some common data that are important to bargaining.

Table 3.1. Basic Provisions of a CBA with Examples.

Contract Provision	Example of the Contract Provision
Recognition	Recognition of union as exclusive representative; identification of the bargaining unit members
Union Rights	Statement of the rights of the union provided in the CBA; organizational security (agency fee); release time for union officers; building uses; mail services
Management Rights	Statement of management rights; usually brackets define some of the limits of the contract and reserves policy-making to the school district
Employee Rights	Review of personnel file; academic freedom, nondiscrimination; environmental concerns; seniority; reduction in force
Job Assignment	Work year; work day hours; assignment; reassignment; transfer; preparation period; teaching load
Evaluations	Purpose; process; intervention assistance
Discipline	Definitions, procedures, remediation, dismissal
Grievances	Definitions, procedures, arbitration (advisory or binding)
Leaves	Sick leave, disability, family, personal, jury duty, military duty, religious, bereavement
Compensation	Salary schedule, additional duty pay, tuition reimbursement
Benefits	health, dental, unemployment, retirement
Contract	Length of contract, reopeners, savings clause if portion of contract is invalidated by a court

Data: Grievances

The grievance log that tracks the history of grievances, management, and labor should each keep a bargaining book in which problems with the contract are recorded and labor relations issues that come up which could be addressed through the contract are also recorded. This information aids in bargaining but may not show directly; but they are influential in deciding what bargaining issues to pursue. Not every labor issue makes it to the bargaining table.

In addition, leadership team meetings should include a section on the agenda to discuss possible and pending grievances. This not only alerts the other school administrators about problems/issues they may soon face, but it also has a centralizing effect in which there is a standard approach to resolving grievances.[17]

This practice brings consistency to the enforcement of the contract and standardization of the contract. It is also a good communication tool in that the immediate supervisor would know if he or she would be supported in his or her response to the grievance at the next level.

For example, in one meeting, an elementary school principal reported on a grievance that was just filed in her school. She told the leadership team what her preferred resolution was and why she wanted to deny the grievance. The grievance was discussed. The director of personnel and labor relations, who was responsible for bargaining and enforcing the contract, concluded the session telling her that she would have to accept the grievance and what the remedy would have to be and why.

The decision was consistent with other similar grievances resolutions and the established practice (standardization and centralization). The principal stated that she believed that she had to follow her course of action to deny the grievance in order to send a specific message. It was agreed that she would not be supported at Level 2 of the grievance.

The great majority, if not all, school districts use a grievance form for the processing of grievances. A log of the grievances is kept to provide an historical perspective for identifying ongoing issues and those which are not ongoing. Copies of the form are not placed in the personnel file of the employee filing the grievance. The union has access to the individual forms and the log upon request.

The grievance log for the simulation is placed in chapter 6. It covers the past five years of grievances. The five-year AWSD grievance log for the simulation is found in chapter 6.

Data: Scattergrams

In order to bargain salary, it is imperative that the school district knows the distribution of employees on the salary schedule. This information is also necessary for the union to know as well. Without this knowledge it is very difficult for either side to discuss any trade proposals that are grounded on facts.

A scattergram is a useful tool for organizing and displaying data on the distribution across the salary schedule. In addition, a school district can use scattergrams as historical data to help ascertain patterns in movement across the columns of the salary schedule so as to forecast increases in salary for budgeting purposes. A sample salary schedule that is used to demonstrate how a scattergram is constructed is shown in table 3.2.

To develop a scattergram, use the vertical column for years (step) and the horizontal columns for education/credits (column) without the actual salary. The same idea holds for the horizontal axis of earned graduate credits. List the number of teachers on each step and column point on the grid. The asterisk means that there are no placements possible for that intersection of year (step) and education (column).Table 3.3 shows the scattergram for the 175 teachers in a sample school district.

The scattergram not only gives the distribution of the faculty on the salary schedule, it also allows for additional data gathering by computing the cost of each column. Scattergram data over time provide information for budget planning such as how long does it typically take a person to move from one track to another.

The template of the scattergram gives administration the ability to look at the relative costs between elementary, middle school, and high school

Table 3.2.   Sample Salary Schedule for Scattergram and Stream of Earnings.

Year	BA	BA+15	MA	MA+15	MA+30
1	34,121	36,466	38,343	41,740	44,520
2	34,529	36,466	40,064	43,183	46,195
3	36,119	38,688	41,909	45,171	48,292
4	37,784	40,467	43,822	47,252	50,519
5	39,513	42,328	45,851	49,424	52,836
6	41,332	44,266	48,004	51,745	55,318
7	43,292	46,363	50,324	54,243	57,985
8	45,273	48,487	52,868	57,084	61,029
9		50,646	55,508	59,554	63,351
10		52,870	59,058	63,584	66,945
11					69,545

Education Stipend—Added to Base Salary—Cumulative
CAGS/CAS/EdS. = $1,000
EdD./PhD. = $2,500
Longevity Stipend—Added to Base Salary and Education Stipend—Noncumulative
12–13 years of continuous service in district = $750
14–16 years of continuous service in district = $1,500
17–19 years of continuous service in district = $2,000
20–25 years of continuous service in district = $2,500
26+ years of continuous service in district = $3,000

Table 3.3. Sample Scattergram Using Sample Salary Schedule.

Year	BA	BA+15	MA	MA+15	MA+30	TOTAL
1	1					1
2		2				2
3	1	1				2
4	1	1				2
5	1	1				2
6		3				3
7	2	2	2			6
8		1	1			2
9		5	5	5		15
10		25	22	15		62
11					78	78
Total	6	41	30	20	78	175

BA = $234,121
BA+15 = $2,043,401
MA = $1,730,332
MA+15 = $1,251,530
MA+30 = $5,424,510
Total Salary = $10,683,894
Stipend for each degree held
CAGS—$1,500 stipend added to salary each year × 18 = $27,000. EdD./PhD.—$2,500 stipend added to salary each year × 7 = $17,500
Longevity Stipend—Added to Base Salary and Education Stipend—Noncumulative
12–13 years of continuous service = $750 × 14 = $10,500
14–16 years of continuous service = $1,500 × 16 = $24,000
17–19 years of continuous service = $2,000 × 17 = 34,000
20–25 years of continuous service = $2,500 × 27 = $67,500
26+ years of continuous service = $3,000 × 69 = $207,000
Total Stipends = $387,500
Grand Total from Salary Schedule = $11,071,394

faculties by developing a scattergram for each level. The template can also be used to disaggregate the data by individual schools.

This scattergram shows that there are a number of teachers (twenty-five) who have not been able to make the jump to the MA column. The MA requirement is possibly presenting an obstacle to column movement.

The union may seek a change to the MA column to one that does not require the MA, such as BA+30/MA. Almost 82 percent of the faculty has twelve or more years of service in the district. This may result in pressure to increase the amount of the longevity stipend, or there may be a push for an additional year (step) on the salary schedule. With seventy-eight teachers (44.6 percent) at the last column, there may be a push for another column, M+45 possibly.

This knowledge allows management to anticipate potential proposals to change the salary schedule, thus giving them time to ascertain if it serves the interests of the district to make a change. For example, adding post-BA units to the MA column may be considered as diminishing an interest in having a faculty with a focused graduate program that master's degree provides as opposed to a collection of possibly unconnected graduate credits.

Data: Stream of Earnings for Comparing Salaries

The ability to compare salary schedules is important for preparing documentation on salary proposals. Linda Kaboolian discusses the benefit of salary benchmarking, a bargaining strategy that may fit well the stream of earnings approach discussed below. Salary benchmarking uses salary schedules from nearby school districts "to set the standard."[18]

This is a two-step process. First, negotiate which school districts will serve as comparators. Second, decide how will the salary schedules be compared? Do the parties use the beginning salary step, the middle/median step and column, or the last step and column? Unfortunately, the process too often becomes an exercise in cherry-picking with each side selecting the point(s) that supports their position as opposed to a search for some objective data.[19]

The stream of earnings approach can be an effective approach mainly because it takes into account salary schedules that are front-loaded in order to attract candidates and end-loaded salary schedules designed to keep employees. It also provides for a way to account for differences in longevity stipends step differentials (maximum number of years on the salary schedule—twelve, fourteen, or fifteen years), and graduate credit differentials (e.g., number of units needed for a track change and when a master's degree is required).

The stream of earnings approach starts with a set of parameters that are applied consistently to the salary schedules being compared. Basically, the earnings of an employee who starts with a school district in his or her first year of employment and stays twenty, twenty-five, or thirty years are tracked. This approach helps to take into account variability of salary schedules. This approach does not describe what the salary schedule should look like. It will help the parties to see the relative fairness of the compared salary schedules.

A sample parameter is shown in the following section. These parameters should change to accurately reflect the pattern of the school district in which bargaining is taking place. The key is for the two sides to agree on the parameters ahead of time. District data on these parameters are very helpful and reduces arguments over what parameters exist in your school district.

Sample Parameters

- The salary schedules selected for comparison do not change for purposes of the analysis. The idea is to keep it simple.

- Employee moves down for each year of service, which will be continual for thirty years.
- Every year the employee accumulates three credits toward column movement on the salary schedule.
- Column movement occurs at the following steps, sixth to BA+15, eleventh to MA, sixteenth to MA+15, and twenty-first to MA+30.
- The teacher receives a master's degree at the eleventh year of employment.

The application of the stream of earnings approach is shown in table 3.4 using a sample salary schedule in Table 3.3.

Table 3.4.   Sample Stream of Earnings Calculation Using Sample Salary Schedule.

Year	Salary	Column Movement (CM) Longevity Stipend (LS)	Salary Subtotal	Running Total
1	34,121			34,121
2	34,529			68,650
3	36,119			104,769
4	37,784			142,553
5	39,513			182,066
6	44,266	CM BA+15		226,332
7	46,363			272,695
8	48,487			321,182
9	50,646			371,828
10	52,870			424,698
11	59,058	CM MA		483,756
12	59,058	LS+750	59,808	543,564
13	59,058	LS+750	59,808	603,372
14	59,058	LS+1,500	60,558	663,930
15	59,058	LS+1,500	60,558	724,488
16	63,584	CM MA+15: LS+1,500	65,084	789,572
17	63,584	LS+2,000	65,584	855,156
18	63,584	LS+2,000	65,584	920,740
19	63,584	LS+2,000	65,584	986,324
20	63,584	LS+2,500	66,084	1,052,408
21	69,545	CM MA+30: LS+2,500	72,045	1,125,453
22	69,545	LS+2,500	72,045	1,196,498
23	69,545	LS+2,500	72,045	1,268,543
24	69,545	LS+2,500	72,045	1,340,588
25	69,545	LS+2,500	72,045	1,412,633
26	69,545	LS+3,000	72,545	1,485,178
27	69,545	LS+3,000	72,545	1,557,723
28	69,545	LS+3,000	72,545	1,630,268
29	69,545	LS+3,000	72,545	1,702,813
30	69,545	LS+3,000	72,545	1,775,358

Start at step one, column one. The salary is $34,121. Keep a running total. For the second year the salary is $34,529 and the running total is $68,650. Move down for the third year to a salary of $36,119 and the total of salary over the three years is $104,769. This same pattern is repeated for years four and five. For year six, the teacher has enough units to move over to the next column BA+15 (column movement). The teacher is now making $44,266 (year six and column BA+15). The running total for the teacher with six years of service is $226,332.

The sample stream of earning completes the thirty years of continuous service. However, comparisons can be made at any point during the thirty years of service. The years of service can also be extended beyond thirty years, but there may not be much of a return on this extra amount of work.

For purposes of the simulation, a stream of earnings can be calculated for AWSD, Metroville School District, and Happy Valley School District salary schedules, comparing the stream of earning at the 20-year, 25-year, and 30-year points.

This method of salary comparisons can be used with most salary schedules to develop comparisons that are truly comparable and not just the product of cherry-picking. Meaningful, reliable, and shared data facilitate negotiations.

Data: Five-Year Comparison for Early Retirement Incentive

School districts often bargain early retirement packages as a means of cutting employee costs, thus saving the school district money. It should not be approached as a reward for service. If that is the goal, it is best to develop a specific reward program, which will likely be very difficult to do if it is linked to merit pay. Also, it is problematic to negotiate an ongoing retirement incentive that an employee can access any year rather than an incentive that has a specific sunset of one year.

Any incentive that management offers will reduce the total savings from the retiring teacher's salary compared to the lower, newly hired teacher's salary. Therefore, the district must find a balance between offering a large enough incentive to induce teachers to retire now rather than waiting for another year or two and making sure that the early retirement incentive plan does not cost the district more than it saves over five years.

Management should approach early retirement incentive packages as a means to save money. The goal is to provide enough of an incentive for a teacher to decide to retire now rather than waiting. A teacher who was going to retire anyway does not save the district money; it costs the district because it is paying an incentive to do something the employee was going to do anyway.

A five-year comparison model provides the employer with information about how much of an incentive can be offered while meeting the goal of saving money (see table 3.5). The comparison assumes no change in the current salary schedule. (Please note that the comparison uses the earlier sample salary schedule in Table 3.2.) The replacement teacher is placed at the Step 1 BA and progresses each year for the following four years. The complete salary cost including fringe benefits is recalculated for each year for the replacement teacher.

The cost difference between the current teacher and the replacement is calculated for five years. It must be remembered that after conducting the five-year comparison between the highest paid faculty member and the replacement costs for a new faculty member, the incentive must be subtracted from the five-year comparison.

- Keeping the current teacher over five years, assuming no raises to the salary schedule, will cost the district $509,455.
- Replacing the current teacher with a first-year teacher, assuming no raises but movement down the salary schedule for each service, will cost the school district $298,453.
- The difference between keeping the current teacher and replacing that teacher over a five-year period is $211,002.

The employer can now find the cost for the incentive that it believes will yield the savings it desires. This also provides the union with important knowledge about costs that can be used for negotiating an early retirement incentive.

Table 3.5.   Five-Year Early Retirement Calculation.

Assumptions	Salary/Fringe
Current Teacher	
Step 11, MA+30	69,545
CAGS	1,000
Longevity 26+years	3,000
Retirement 5.8%	4,208
Federal Insurance Contributions Act (FICA) 7.65%	5,550
Salary Total	83,303
Dental Single+1	744
Kaiser Single+1	17,100
Disability Insurance	300
Life Insurance 0.21/1,000 salary	15 (73.545 × 0.21 = 15.44)
Worker's Compensation 0.54/100	397 (735.45 × 0.54 = 397.14)
Unemployment	32
Fringe Benefit Total	$18,588
Grand Total	$101,891

Replacement Teacher—Year One	Salary and Fringe
Step 1, BA	34,121
Retirement 5.8%	1,979
FICA 7.65%	2,610
Salary Total	$38,710
Dental Single+1	744
Kaiser Single+1	17,100
Disability Insurance	300
Life Insurance 0.21/1,000 Salary	7 (34.121 × 0.21 = 7.17)
Worker's Compensation 0.54/100	184 (341.21 × 0.54 = 184.25)
Unemployment	32
Fringe Benefit Total	$18,367
Grand Total	$57,077

Replacement Teacher—Year Two	Salary and Fringe
Step 2, BA	34,529
Retirement 5.8%	2,003
FICA 7.65%	2,641
Salary Total	$39,173

Assumptions	Salary/Fringe
Dental Single+1 Kaiser Single +1 Disability Insurance	744
	17,100
	300
Life Insurance 0.21/1,000 Salary	7 (34.529 × 0.21 = 7.25)
Worker's Compensation 0.54/100	186 (345.29 × 0.54 = 186.46)
Unemployment	32
Fringe Benefit Total	$18,369
Grand Total	$57,542

Replacement Teacher—Year Three	Salary and Fringe
Step 3, BA	36,119
Retirement 5.8%	2,095
FICA 7.65%	2,763
Salary Total	$40,977
Dental Single+1	744
Kaiser Single+1	17,100
Disability Insurance	300
Life Insurance 0.21/1,000 Salary	8 (36.119 × 0.21 = 7.58)
Worker's Compensation 0.54/100	195 (361.19 × 0.54 = 195.04)
Unemployment	32
Fringe Benefit Total	$18,379
Grand Total	$59,356

(Continued)

Table 3.5. Continued

Replacement Teacher—Year Four	Salary and Fringe
Step 4, BA	37,784
Retirement 5.8%	2,191
FICA 7.65%	2,890
Salary Total	$42,865
Dental Single+1	744
Kaiser Single+1	17,100
Disability Insurance	300

Assumptions	Salary/Fringe
Life Insurance 0.21/1,000 Salary	8 (37.784 × 0.21 = 7.93)
Worker's Compensation 0.54/100	204 (377.84 × 0.54 = 204.03)
Unemployment	32
Fringe Benefit Total	$18,388
Grand Total	$61,253

Replacement Teacher—Year Five	Salary and Fringe
Step 5, BA	39,513
Retirement 5.8%	2,292
FICA 7.65%	3,023
Salary Total	$44,828
Dental Single+1	744
Kaiser Single+1	17,100
Disability Insurance	300
Life Insurance 0.21/1,000 Salary	8 (39.513 × 0.21 = 8.30)
Worker's Compensation 0.54/100	213 (395.13 × 0.54 = 213.37)
Unemployment	32
Fringe Benefit Total	$18,397
Grand Total	$63,225

Data: Review of the Contract

Another piece of important data for preparation for bargaining is a review of the current CBA. The following questions may help to focus the analysis of the contract. It is also a worthwhile practice for new administrators to a school district to carefully review the CBA particularly noting critical deadlines. These questions can also be assigned to graduate students in a labor relations course to apply these questions to their school district's CBA.

Contract Analysis Questions

1. Which positions are covered by the CBA? This constitutes the bargaining unit. Are there any employees who are left out of the bargaining unit and who believe may be part of the community of interest that originally formed the union?

2. Are the rights of the union robust and expansive or are they narrowly drawn?
3. Is the definition of a grievance narrow and specific to alleged violations of the CBA or is it broad and/or vague? How is the definition applied broadly or narrowly (review the grievance log)?
4. Does the contract have advisory or binding arbitration? Are there any sections of the contract that are excluded (positive assurance) from arbitration?
5. List the steps for processing a grievance—filed to whom? Number of days for a response?
6. Can the content of an observation of teaching be grieved?
7. Can the content of an evaluation be grieved?
8. What restrictions, if any, are in the contract concerning faculty meetings and after-school meetings? Are these restrictions reasonable from an administrator's point of view?
9. What restrictions, if any, are in the contract concerning classroom observations? Are these restrictions reasonable from an administrator's point of view?
10. Do teachers automatically proceed to the next step for a year of service on the salary schedule, or is there a qualification on the automatic step increase?
11. What changes, if any, would you recommend that the school board initiate in the next round of bargaining?

Ready to Bargain

The earlier discussion provides a beginning approach to preparing to sit at the table. It is not exhaustive, but it is instructive. What other questions about preparation do these factors and data raise for consideration of additional data?

The next chapter discusses what happens at the table. It will start with the essential requirement to approach bargaining in good faith.

Table 3.6.   Savings over Five Years Comparing Current Teacher with Replacement Teacher.

Year	Current Teacher Salary and Fringe	Replacement Salary and Fringe	Teacher Difference	Yearly Total Difference
1	101,891	57,077	44,814	44,814
2	101,891	57,542	44,349	89,163
3	101,891	59,356	42,535	131,698
4	101,891	61,253	40,638	172,336
5	101,891	63,225	38,666	211,002

NOTES

1. Frederick M. Hess and Martin R. West, *A Better Bargain: Overhauling Teacher Collective Bargaining for the 21st Century* (Cambridge, MA: Harvard University, Program on Education Policy and Governance, March 29, 2006), 9.

2. Roger Fisher and Danny Ertel, *Getting Ready to Negotiate: The Getting to Yes Workbook* (New York: Penguin Books, 1995), 96.

3. Ibid., 3.

4. Hess and West, *A Better Bargain*, 9.

5. William G. Keane, *Win Win or Else: Collective Bargaining in an Age of Public Discontent* (Thousand Oaks, CA: Corwin Press, Inc., 1996), 4.

6. Todd A. DeMitchell and Thomas Carroll, "Educational Reform on the Bargaining Table: Impact, Security, and Tradeoffs." *Education Law Reporter* 134 (1999): 675–93, 687.

7. Myron Lieberman, *The Teacher Unions: How the NEA and AFT Sabotage Reform and Hold Students, Parents, Teachers, and Taxpayers Hostage to Bureaucracy* (New York: The Free Press, 1997), 47.

8. *Indian River County Education Association, Local 3617 v. School Board of India River County*, 4 FPER 4262 (1978), *aff'd*, 373 So. 2d 412 (Fla. 4th DCA 1979).

9. Michael Hansen (March 17, 2009), "State Intervention an Contract Choice in the Public Teacher Labor Market." In Stephen Sawchuck (April 6, 2009), "Researchers Examine Contracts' Effects on Policy Issues." *Education Week*. Visited May 4, 2009, available at http://www.edweek.org/ew/articles/2009/04/08/28bargain_ep.h28.html, p. 2.

10. McNeil Stokes, "Labor Relations: Permissive Subject of Bargaining." Visited December 8, 2008, available at http://www.acwi.org/cd/pdfs/7705_x.pdf.

11. David P. Twomey, *Labor Law and Legislation* (7th Ed.) (Cincinnati, OH: South-Western Publishing Co., 1985), 501.

12. *Ridgefield Park Education Association v. Ridgefield Park Board of Education*, 393 A.2d 278, 287 (N.J. 1978).

13. *Aberdeen Education Association v. Aberdeen Board of Education*, 215 N.W.2d 837, 841 (S.D. 1974).

14. *AFGE Local 32*, 51 FLRA 491, 507 (1995).

15. For a discussion of the requirement to bargain the impact of the decision to transfer bargaining unit work outside of the bargaining unit, see Commonwealth Employment Relations Board (Massachusetts) case, *In the Matter of Board of Higher Education and American Federation of State, County and Municipal Employees Council 93, AFL-CIO, Local 1067*, Case No. SUP-08–5453 (February 14, 2014).

16. Seattle Public Schools, "Collective Bargaining Agreement." Visited July 1, 2017, available at http://www.seattleschools.org/cms/One.aspx?portalId=627&pageId=15568.

17. For a discussion on formalizing, standardizing, and centralizing relationships, see Todd A. DeMitchell, *Labor Relations in Education Policies, Politics, and Practices* (Lanham, MD: Rowman & Littlefield Education, 2010).

18. Linda Kaboolian, *Win-Win Labor Management Collaboration in Education: Breakthrough Practices to Benefit Students, Teachers, and Administrators* (Mt. Morris, IL: Education Week Press, 2005), 24.

19. This concern is supported by research by Linda Babcock, Xianghong Wang, and George Lowenstein, "Choosing the Wrong Pond: Social Comparisons in Negotiations that Reflect a Self-Serving Bias" *The Quarterly Journal of Economics* 111 (1996): 1–18, who found that school districts and unions in Pennsylvania chose comparison groups in ways that advanced their positions rather than providing neutral data points to support bargaining.

Chapter 4

At the Table

A "no" uttered from the deepest conviction is better than a greater "yes" merely uttered to please, or worse to avoid trouble.[1]

—Mahatma Gandhi

Collective bargaining means more than the discussion of individual problems and grievances with employees or groups of employees. It means that the employer is obligated to negotiate in good faith with his employees as a group, through their representatives.

—Atlantic Refining Company, 1 N.L.R.B. 359, 368 (1935)

GOOD FAITH AT THE TABLE

Bargaining is the central activity of a union and a critical part of labor relations, in general. The preparation for bargaining reviewed in the previous chapter is a prelude to the bargaining that takes place at the table. This chapter discusses what happens at the table.

Essentially, there are three types of bargaining. There is the general legal requirement for both parties to bargain in good faith, discussed in more detail later. Bad faith bargaining is the absence of good faith. There is also hard bargaining in which one side or the other takes a strong position, defends that position, but also keeps a mind accessible to persuasion to other options. Hard bargaining does not mean bad faith bargaining. The third type is surface bargaining in which the party goes through the motions with no real intent on trying to reach an agreement.

Good faith arose in the first half of the twentieth century when the National Labor Relations Board (NLRB) "perceived inequitable bargaining status between unions and employers."[2] Good faith does not require that either side acquiesce to the demands of the other or that the two sides try to meet in the middle. For example, the NLRB wrote, "If honest and sincere bargaining efforts fail to produce an understanding on terms, nothing in the Act makes illegal the employer's refusal to accept terms submitted to him."[3]

The legal requirement, consistently found in both public-sector and private-sector collective bargaining, is that each side must bargain in good faith. The requirement to bargain in good faith is the cornerstone of collective bargaining, both public and private. But what is good faith?

There is a mutual obligation on the part of management and labor to bargain in good faith. Typically, the law requires both management and labor to meet at reasonable times and to confer in good faith with respect to wages, hours, and other terms and conditions of employment. This obligation does not compel either party to agree to a proposal or require them to make a concession. Both sides coming to the table as equals is a good beginning point for good faith. The practical rules for bargaining in good faith are as follows:

- Approach bargaining with a mind accessible to persuasion.
- Follow procedures that will enhance the prospects of a negotiated settlement.
- Be willing to discuss freely and fully your respective claims and demands. When such claims and demands are opposed by the other side, be prepared to justify your claims with reason.
- Explore with an open mind proposals for compromise or other possible solutions of differences. Make an effort to find a mutually satisfactory basis for agreement.

The purpose of collective bargaining is to "bring to the bargaining table parties willing to present their proposals and articulate supporting reasons, to listen to weigh the proposals and reasons of the other party, and to search for some common ground which can serve as the basis for a written bilateral agreement."[4] The requirement to bargain in good faith is found consistently in state collective bargaining law,[5] as well as in the National Labor Relations Board Act.[6] Consequently, the failure to bargain in good faith is an ULP—a violation of the law.

An interesting case arose in Missouri in which the Supreme Court of Missouri in *American Federation of Teachers v. Lebetter* (2012) was faced with the question whether Missouri Constitution required school districts to bargain in good faith.[7] Article I, section 29 of the Missouri Constitution provides that "employees shall have the right to organize and to bargain collectively through representatives of their own choosing."[8] This applies to both public- and private-sector employees. However, Missouri does not have any statutory language imposing a duty to bargain in good faith.

The court asserted that without a duty to negotiate in good faith, the constitutional right under Article I section 29 "would be nullified or redundant." If public employers had no duty to bargain in good faith, they could virtually act with impunity, thus thwarting collective bargaining by never genuinely seeking to reach agreement—"frustrating the very purpose of bargaining and invalidating the right."[9] School districts and exclusive representatives must negotiate in good faith in Missouri even without authorizing language. The Court upheld the principle that collective bargaining is predicated on approaching the table with a mind accessible to persuasion and with an earnest endeavor to reasonably find the common interests for a negotiated settlement.

TEXT BOX 4.1

The duty [to bargain collectively] encompasses an obligation to enter into discussion and negotiation with a fair mind and with a sincere purpose to find agreement.

—Highland Park Manufacturing Company, 12 N.L.R.B. 1238, 1248–49 (1939).

Violations of good faith bargaining typically fall into one of two categories: *per se* on *totality of conduct.* A per se violation involves conduct on the part of one party that establishes a prima facie case of bad faith. It is conduct that is considered proof of the party's objective to evade its duty to bargain. These types of violations are found without regard to the presence or absence of subjective good faith. *Per se violations* include:[10]

- Making unilateral changes and refusal to bargain. Under the National Labor Relations Act (NLRA), the unilateral changes must be material, substantial, or significant;[11]
- Delaying or conditioning bargaining; and
- Insistence to impasse upon a permissive subject of bargaining constitutes.
- Interference with a party's selection of bargaining team members.
- Bypassing a bargaining team's selected negotiators. This is often called direct dealing. "The Obligation to bargain in good faith requires at a minimum recognition that the statutory representative is the one with whom the employer must deal in conducting bargaining negotiations, and that it can no longer bargain directly or indirectly with the employees."[12] Management cannot offer inducements, or be coercive, thus bypassing the exclusive representative. However, the employer can communicate directly with its employees and accurately inform them of the terms of its collective bargaining proposals.[13]

- Unions may also be involved in bad faith bargaining by bypassing the school district's representative. In Washington state, the Kiona Benton Education Association breached the duty to bargain in good faith when it refused to communicate with the school district's representative and stated that it would only communicate with the superintendent.[14]
- Refusal to discuss economic matters until agreement on all noneconomic matters has been reached.
- Refusal to execute a written agreement embodying terms which the parties had reached agreement.
- Repudiating the tentatively signed agreements.
- Refusal to provide pertinent information.
- A request for information that involves wages and benefits carries a heavy presumption of relevance.
- If the union requests fall outside the ambit of wages and benefits, the union carries the burden of demonstrating pertinence.
- There is no obligation that the requested material must be presented in any form that the union requests.

TEXT BOX 4.2

BOULWARISM: A WELL-KNOWN EXAMPLE OF BAD FAITH BARGAINING

Lemuel Boulware was the vice president for General Electric in the 1960s. He would closely consider the union's demands, evaluate the workers' needs through a survey (a form of direct dealing), the competition's wages and working conditions, and ability of the company to meet those needs and issue, in his words, a "fair, firm offer" with nothing held back for future concessions or negotiations. Boulware asserted that he was placing the "first, last, and best offer" on the table. He then refused to make any counterproposals, thus ending negotiations. This approach came to be known as a "take it or leave it" offer or a counteroffer, or "Boulwarism." The NLRB considered it bad faith bargaining.[*]

[*] For interesting law review articles on Boulwarism, see Morriss D. Forkosch, "Boulwarism: Will Labor-Management Relations Take It or Leave It?"19 *Catholic University Law Review* 311 (1970), and for a response from one of the union representatives, see Irving Abramson, "The Anatomy of Boulwarism with a Discussion of Forkosch" 19 *Catholic University Law Review* 459 (1970).

- The employer only has to provide information that it actually has in its possession. It does not have to research or access other databases in order to provide the information that the union wants when the employer has accessed the information for their purposes. In other words, the employer cannot be transformed into the research arm of the union to search out whatever information the union wants.

The totality of conduct test looks to the entire course of negotiations to determine the party's subjective intent. It is the essence of surface bargaining that a party goes through the motions of negotiations, but in fact is weaving otherwise unobjectionable conduct into an entangling fabric meant to delay or prevent agreement.

The following are some factors that have been found to be indicative of bad faith bargaining under *the totality of conduct test*:

- Frequent turnover in negotiators.
- Negotiator's lack of authority which delays or thwarts the bargaining process.[15]
- Lack of preparation for bargaining sessions.
- Missing, delaying, or canceling bargaining sessions.
- Insistence on ground rules before negotiating substantive issues.
- Taking an inflexible position.
- Regressive bargaining proposals.
- Predictably unacceptable counterproposals.

As stated earlier, but worth stating again, good faith bargaining does not compel either side to meet the other part way. It does not require that concessions be made; the difference between the sides does not have to split so that they meet in the middle. Making a concession may not serve the interests of your constituency. Hard bargaining in which one side says "no" does not equate to bad faith. At times, "no" can be the better, the more appropriate response.

However, just a "no" without an explanation as to why and how the interests of your constituency are not met can move the needle toward bad faith bargaining. Similar to any proposal that is brought to the table, but especially if the proposal was unacceptable, a good faith approach is to start with questions first to help understand the proposal and to underscore some of the problems with the proposal.

After exploration of the proposal and it is clear that it will not work as presented to say, "as your proposal currently stands, we cannot accept it" followed by reasons for the statement is not bad faith. However, if a spokesperson believes that the proposal may be workable and consistent with his/her practices and interests, the proposal can be taken under advisement to resurface at a later time for discussion.

Closely read the language of the proposal. Listen carefully to the other side's reason for the proposal. What interests does it serve? Ask questions about the proposal to clear up ambiguities and inconsistencies. Ask questions that are designed to ascertain if the proposal fits your interests. If you find that the proposal is not in the best interests of the constituency who you represent at the table, say no.

For example, a school district had serious financial problems and was approaching bargaining. The problem was compounded by the fact that the salary and benefits of the school district were considered to be a very high, but no longer sustainable at the same level of increases offered in the past. The teachers had come to expect a good salary raise that would allow them to keep their high position with neighboring school districts.

With this backdrop, the school district began negotiating a new contract. Every monetary item that came to the table resulted in the management's spokesperson asking whether the net effect of the proposal would increase the long-term indebtedness or help to solve the financial problem. Each proposal from the teachers union and from the classified employees union was reviewed with this consideration in mind. The district bargained hard but approached each proposal in good faith to see if it would meet the district's interests or hinder those interests.

However, only bargaining in good faith during negotiations is no substitute for a lack of good faith during the year. The true measure of success of bargaining is not securing an agreement; success is when the relations between the parties improves, or at least does not deteriorate. Good faith should be a description of an ongoing process of good relations between educators.

Fisher and Ury in *Getting to Yes* pose the following questions as a means of getting at acting in good faith:

- Is this an approach I would use with my good friends or family?
- Would I be embarrassed if a full account of my actions were printed in the local newspaper?
- If this were a book, would I be cast as the hero or villain?[16]

Both *Getting to Yes* and *Getting Together* are discussed in chapter 2.

Good faith bargaining, hopefully leads to an "elegant" negotiation solution, a term used by David Kuechle, professor emeritus, Graduate School of Education, Harvard University. Professor Richard Fossey at the University of Louisiana at Lafayette developed the following elegant solution.

AN ELEGANT SOLUTION

1. The solution is better than any party's BATNA.
2. All parties are committed to making the solution work.

3. The solution produces a good working relationship.
4. The solution is appropriate for long-term goals.
5. The solution can feasibly be implemented.
6. There is a clear understanding between the parties as to the meaning of the solution.
7. No joint interests are remaining to be addressed.
8. The process by which the agreement is achieved is seen by all parties as fair.[17]

THE BARGAINING TEAM AT THE BARGAINING TABLE

There is no one best way to organize a bargaining team. There is no consistent empirical research that points to the best organization. With this limitation in mind, the following is meant to spark a discussion and to raise questions. They are not meant to be the definitive answer. The following observations may work for some but may not work for all.

These thoughts on bargaining are offered for consideration.

- *You bargain with three groups*—your team, the other team, and your constituency, either the school board or the union's leadership council.

Some of the most difficult bargaining can be with your team and the constituency whom you represent at the table. Bargaining with a team takes place in caucus sessions when proposals, as well as responses to the other side's proposals, are developed. These discussions focus on strategies—what was working, what was not working. These discussions need to be open, unrestrained, and freewheeling. In the give-and-take of these negotiations on how to proceed, the team was at its best when it gives its unvarnished opinion and questioned each other and me. The chief spokesperson is responsible for negotiations and must consider their comments, warnings, and suggestions. No surprises is a good maxim.

Most often constituency bargaining takes place in a closed session with the school board or the union's leadership team. Bargaining with a school board or a union leadership team over interests that are being served by bargaining include the impact of the monetary sections of the contract. If the spokesperson is a hired professional with expertise in negotiations, the school board and union leadership team have the more powerful position as policymakers. They also have the responsibility to make the contract work in the schools.

In bargaining, data and persuasiveness are used to steer the constituency in the direction that the superintendent of union president believe is best. For those who have worked with school boards, they know the delicate dance over limits of board action that administrators do with school board members. The spokesperson must know the limits and the interests that must be pursued after the negotiation, as well as during negotiations.

The third bargaining party sits at the other side of the table.

• *The chief spokesperson does the talking at the table.* While it is important for the bargaining team to have ample opportunity to take part in the process during our caucus negotiations, one person representing a side can better control the flow of the conversation and keep it on track. Only one person at a time can drive the car, and a chief spokesperson best meets the responsibility to be the GPS system that keeps the team moving in the right direction. When there are too many hands on the wheel, the result is an erratic, lurching journey. The follow-up question is, if the chief spokesperson is doing the talking, what is the rest of team doing?

An important role team members undertake is to take notes during the negotiations. When one side receives a proposal from the other team, all members of the receiving team need to read it carefully and ask any questions regarding the proposal so that everyone thoroughly understands the proposal, its possible impact, raising potential problems with the proposal. This takes place at the bargaining table. This is an important team action. The better the understanding of the proposal, its ramifications, and how it serves the other side's interests, the better is the chance that a community of interest can be found that helps both sides to meet their interests.

A close reading of the proposal accompanied by questions seeking understanding of the proposal is a good communication strategy. Questions are also a good way to signal problems that you may have with the proposal in a less adversarial way. The give-and-take of questions and answers about a proposal can have a positive impact on table talk.

Team members are *not* assigned to watch a member of the other team. It is a waste of time to look for some signs that tells what the other side is thinking. Time can be better used in keeping accurate notes and participating in the discussion on the other side's proposals when appropriate. Listening to the other side and carefully reading their proposals tell us more about their intentions and interests than facial expressions. The effectiveness of table talk should drive the decision and not the individual's need to talk.

• *The team needs broad representation.* Including a representative from each school level on the bargaining team is a good strategy. Too often ideas that make sense at the bargaining table when discussing issues that need a resolution fail to meet the requirements of the real world of the school. Adding principals or assistant principals to the team helps to keep the table talk and proposals grounded in the reality of the school where the contract is implemented and enforced.[18]

• *Keep the white horse in the stable and white knight at the round table and not at the bargaining table.* Beware of the white knight on the white horse riding in to join the table talk with the solution that will result in a contract. There sometimes is the urge for someone with power who is not at the table to want to come in at the eleventh hour to "save" the contract by offering "the" solution. School board members, superintendents, and union presidents often want to mount up to save the day. While it may be satisfying for the individual, it is rarely effective in the long run.

Once the knight has ridden up to the table, the dynamic shifts and the flow of negotiations changes. A potential backdoor to negotiations could possibly have been opened. The other team may believe that only having the knight at the table could get them what they want and consequently defer substantive discussions.

Bargaining is hard work. It involves building trust. If there is a perception that someone from outside the table can ride in, be it a school board member or a superintendent, the table will be in expectation of their arrival. Power shifts away from the table/team when the perceived real problem-solver waits for entry to the room. It is hard for leaders to stay away from the bargaining table, but they should either be at the table for the long haul or they should wait and fill their role allowing the bargaining team to do its job.

PROPOSALS, SUPPOSALS, AND THE WATER COOLER

A proposal is a written document exchanged with the other party at the bargaining table. It is language intended to be used in the contract being bargained. It is the major way in which the parties at the bargaining table trade and discuss what they are seeking in the contract. Contract language contained in the proposal seeks clarity and transparency. A good rule of thumb is borrowed from substantive due process analysis; would the reasonable person know what to do or what not to do upon reading the language of the proposal?

Policy often works best with some ambiguity, some vagueness, some wiggle room; contract language does not. Contract language must be explicit, direct, clear, and simple.

When preparing a proposal, it is not necessary to restate every section that currently exists in the contract for which you are not requesting a change. Designating sections that are unchanged simply as "no change" can be efficient. This has the added benefit of directing attention to the changes in the current contract. The goal of proposals is to be clear about intentions and language. This is important as an overall strategy of improving labor relations. To hide the impact of language is to invite retaliation in the next round of negotiations and there is always another round of negotiations. Trust is built on openness; it is injured through deception.

The following is an example of a proposal using the AWSD simulation (see chapter 6).[19] Note that the upper-left-hand corner of the proposal has the date and time when the proposal was offered. It also designates that it is a management proposal and it states that it is management's second proposal on this contract section. This is important for keeping track of the proposals.

District #2
3/25/20XX
3:46 pm

ARTICLE 9

Class Size

9.1 General

The following class sizes shall be defined as applicable for all schools in the District:

Grades: K   25
Grades 1–3   26
Grades 4–5   27
Grades 6–12   30 with the exception of science laboratories which shall have a maximum of 24 students.

9.2 Combination classes

The class size for elementary classes, which combine one or more grade levels shall be reduced by one. The lower class size shall be used as the base for the reduction in class size.

9.3 Preparation time for middle and high school—no change

9.4 300 minutes of preparation time every ten work days—no change

9.5 Student class assignments

Student class assignments shall be made by the principal or his/her designee. If student class assignments have been made by that would go over the class size limits stated in 9.1, the principal, or designee, shall follow the procedures below:

9.51 No change

9.52 No change

9.53 If the foregoing approaches do not work to bring the class size into the prescribed limits stated above, the District may choose to implement the class size bonus plan below or hire a teacher to reduce the adversely affected class size.

  A A teacher who exceeds the maximum class size for ten (10) consecutive days shall on the eleventh (11) consecutive day be paid ten (10) dollars per day per student over the maximum, retroactive back to the first day the class size maximum was exceeded. The District may end this practice in an individual classroom by reducing the class size to the prescribed maximum or less.

  B There will be a period during the first three weeks of the semester in which 9.53 A will not be in effect so as to allow the District the ability to move students.

  C The District shall place no more than two students over the class size limit in any one class.

  D The class size stipend will not be calculated into the base salary and shall remain a bonus. The affected teacher shall be paid once a month for the class size bonus.

  E Teachers affected by this class size bonus shall complete all district-generated paperwork in accordance with reasonable timelines.

Both spokespersons signing the end of the document with the date and initialing every page with the date with an original for each party is a prudent practice. The goal is to allow as little room as possible between the last line and the signature/initials.

Another type of proposal is a packaged proposal. This type of proposal ties one or more sections of the contract together. For example, using the AWSD simulation, a packaged proposal could include early retirement, salary, and grievance language. It is important that both sides realize that a package proposal is cut from whole cloth. It cannot be separated out with the other party stating that it will accept, for example, the grievance section but not the other parts and expect that the packaged proposal would bind the moving party. The packaged proposal is accepted as a package or not at all. Packaged proposals tend to work best toward the end of negotiations rather than at the beginning. It is important to package proposals so that both parties can see the relationship between the sections and the overall interests of the parties.

Talking at the Table

The bargaining table is designed for talk and is not just a flat surface for passing proposals. Therefore, the type of talk that takes place at the table is important.

It helps to develop trust and defines the quality and interest in personal relations; it provides the place for the human element of collective bargaining (see chapter 2). The two sides talk to each other, most times civilly but not always. Passion can run high because issues of power and worth lurk just below the surface of the discussion. The quality of the table talk—defined as the conversations that take place when representatives from both labor and management sit together at the bargaining table—and the quality of the proposals impact the outcome of bargaining.

Michael Jette, assistant superintendent, Bedford School District, New Hampshire, studied table talk at New Hampshire public school bargaining sessions for his doctoral dissertation at the University of New Hampshire. He found that both teacher union leaders and school superintendents in his study believed that table talk impacted the outcome of bargaining. Almost 94 percent of the union leaders and 91 percent of the management team leaders described their table talk as either extremely related or related to the outcome of bargaining.

One of the issues that Dr. Jette focused on was whether the table talk was primarily debate or dialogue, using Berman's construct of public conversations.[20] Adapting Berman's construct to the collective bargaining table, Jette posed some of the following debate/dialogue paired statements in which respondents were asked to choose their position along a continuum between the statements:

Debate "Our 'table talk' sought to find flaws and counter arguments."
Dialogue "Our 'table talk' sought to understand, find meaning and find agreement."
Debate "The 'table talk' put forward our best thinking, and defended it against challenge to show that it was right."
Dialogue "The 'table talk' put forth our best thinking, knowing that the reflections of others would only help to improve rather than to destroy it."[21]

Jette also found a moderate correlation ($p = .320$) for both labor and management together between the dialogue/debate score and success of bargaining—the greater the dialogue, the greater is the success, and the greater the dialogue, the lesser is the success.[22]

In addition, he found that respondents who reported their bargaining to be unsuccessful or highly unsuccessful tended to report that the table talk was "oppositional," "an attempt to prove the other side wrong," and the table talk was used to defend against challenge and to show their side was "right," the parties failed to listen to each other, and the people were belittled or offended.[23]

A supposal uses table talk; it is not a proposal in the traditional sense. A proposal is a formal statement with a written component, whereas a supposal is an invitation to explore options. It starts with "what if we." It allows the parties to brainstorm and explore without feeling that either side is constrained by the formality of a proposal. This is effective in breaking out of the rut of just trading written proposals with little to no discussion. This allows for bargaining to be the problem-solving activity as DeMitchell and Barton found that the more bargaining was viewed as problem-solving, the less it was viewed as "an obstacle to reform."[24] It also can be an opportunity for dialogue as opposed to debate.

Water cooler negotiation is the last form of negotiations. Water cooler negotiations are informal conversations that take place away from the table between the chief negotiators of both parties. One side calling a caucus and then suggesting that his or her counterpart looks thirsty typically initiates these conversations. This is meant as an invitation to have a conversation away from the table.

Water cooler negotiations can work when one of the two sides wants to "float" some idea that can break the stalemate that has occurred at the table. It is similar to a supposal except that it takes place away from the table and is between the chief negotiators, whereas supposals occur at the table with both teams. The danger of this strategy is that either bargaining team could believe that a private deal was being discussed that bypassed them. Suspicions and concerns must be addressed by the spokesperson and is part of the bargaining that goes on within teams.

This can be an effective strategy but it must be used sparingly. It provides an informal opportunity to explore options that may result in a formal proposal. It must also be used in such a way that your bargaining team does not lose its trust in the chief spokesperson, thinking that they are left out of the bargaining and thus have no importance in the process.

Water cooler negotiations work best when the discussion at the water cooler is brought back to the respective teams for further discussion. From there, they may be brought to the table. To treat water cooler negotiations as the same as a proposal may harm the informality of this type of negotiations in the future. Water cooler negotiations can be a valuable strategy, but it should not be overused. Also, unless it is brought to the table it should be used as a lever at the table backing the other party into corner.

MANAGING INFORMATION

Bargaining often involves handling large amounts of information. How to manage that data in a meaningful way that facilitates bargaining is a challenge. A multifaceted approach is best. Management of data helps to keep bargaining moving forward; it provides a basis for comparing proposals; it provides a record of intentions, and it provides a record for possible ULP charges and arbitration hearings. Another important reason for managing information is that a bargaining team never wants to counter its own proposal. Keeping track of which side presented a proposal last helps to avoid this cardinal bargaining sin. It is important but too often it is approached in a haphazard manner. The following is an approach that has been used at the table.

Minutes

As stated earlier, all members of the bargaining team can and should take notes for each bargaining session. They should try to capture the table talk, identify who is at the table, and track the approximate of the passage of time. All of the notes from the team can be gathered. From those notes, the official minutes is drafted. The draft is shared with the team for accuracy. Once agreement has been reached, the working minutes notes are destroyed and one set of official minutes is kept. This set of official minutes for each bargaining session is then used for all subsequent negotiations and any subsequent legal proceedings, such as arbitration and ULPs. The process strives for the greatest accuracy possible.

A copy of the minutes can be placed in spokesperson's bargaining binder for referral at the table. The original signature and date can be kept in the bargaining file. One copy is used for current negotiations and the original is used for historical reference and future use. Do not underestimate the power of a written document. Minutes are written for three audiences—your side, the other side, and a neutral third party (arbitration, ULPs, and/or a court proceeding). The minutes are not distributed to the other side. However, they can be quoted from to make a point at the table.

Proposals

Proposals for specific contract sections are numbered and kept together. Similarly, packaged proposals are also kept together numerically. A three-ring binder with each section of the contract tabbed is a good organizational tool that is brought to the table by the spokesperson. The first sheet is the existing contract language. Following the original, each proposal is placed in order of presentation. If the union proposal is not numbered, dated, and timed, those notations can be added. This allows the team to see the progression of bargaining on an individual section of the contract. Packaged proposals are identified in a separate section of the bargaining binder.

Tentative Agreements

All originals of the TA along with the minutes are kept in a locked fireproof file cabinet. A copy of the TAs and the minutes can be kept in a second bargaining book that can be brought to the table.

Overall Bargaining

At the front of the three-ring bargaining binder, a contract master list places each contract section vertically on the left-hand margin. Horizontally, place a series of columns with alternating titles of district and union with room for the date of the meeting. For each contract section enter the number of the proposal for each side. When a section has been signed off as a tentative agreement, write TA in capital letters.

This contract list is important for keeping track of where each section is in bargaining. Periodically review the list with the other team to make sure that there is agreement on what has been TAed and what has not. There is nothing worse than one side believing that a contract has reached a TA and the other does not. It is prudent to check with the other side. If there is a disagreement, use the second bargaining book with a copy of the TA section and the minutes that recorded the TA.

Chapter 2 discusses an approach to bargaining building on recognizing a conflict of interests and capitalizing on the community interest. It provides an orientation for developing and keeping relationships and a framework for finding agreement. Chapter 3 focuses on the important work of preparing for bargaining. This chapter has looked at what happens at the bargaining table. Together, they provide a foundation for the last chapter, which offers suggestions and raises questions for bargaining the AWSD simulation (chapter 6).

NOTES

1. William Ury, *The Power of a Positive No: How to Say No and Still Get to Yes* (New York: Bantam, 2007), 7.

2. Marc Manelman and Kevin Manara, "Staying above the Surface—Surface Bargaining Claims under the National Labor Relations Act." *Hofstra Labor & Employment Law Journal* 24 (2007): 261–93, 263.

3. *Inland Steel Company*, 9 N.L.R.B. 783, 797 (1938).

4. Robert A. Gorman, *Basic Text on Labor Law: Unionization and Collective Bargaining* (St. Paul, MN: West Publishing Co., 1976), 399.

5. For an example of the legislative requirement to bargain in good faith in New Hampshire, see RSA 273-A:3 Obligation to Bargain—I. It is the obligation of the public employer and the employee organization certified by the board as the exclusive representative of the bargaining unit to negotiate in good faith. "Good faith" negotiation involves meeting at reasonable times and places in an effort to reach agreement on the terms of employment, and to cooperate in mediation and fact-finding required by this chapter, but the obligation to negotiate in good faith shall not compel either party to agree to a proposal or to make a concession.

Furthermore, in Illinois the public-sector collective bargaining reads in pertinent part: P.A. 84–832 Section 10 Duty to bargain. (a) An educational employer and the exclusive representative have the authority and the duty to bargain collectively as set forth in this section. Collective bargaining is the performance of the mutual obligations of the educational employer and the representative of the educational employees to meet at reasonable times and confer in good faith with respect to wages, hours, and other terms and conditions of employment, and to execute a written contract incorporating any agreement reached by such obligation, provided such obligation does not compel either party to agree to a proposal or require the making of a concession.

6. National Labor Relations Act, 29 USCA 158(d).

7. *American Federation of Teachers v. Ledbetter*, 387 S.W.3d 360, 362 (Missouri 2012) (*en banc*).

8. Ibid., 363.

9. Ibid., 364.

10. American Bar Association (n.d.), "Management and Union's Rights and Obligations in Collective Bargaining," 1. Visited May 5, 2016, available at http://www.americanbar.org/content/dam/aba/events/labor_law/basics_papers/nlra/obligations.authcheckdam.pdf.

11. See *Falcon Wheel Division*, 338 N.L.R.B. 576 (2002).

12. American Bar Association, "Management and Union's Rights and Obligations in Collective Bargaining," 3.

13. See *Emhardt Industries, Hartford Division*, 297 N.L.R.B. 215 (1987).

14. *Kiona Benton School District v. Kiona Benton Education Association*, Decision 11862-A (EDUC, 2014). The Commission held that the union interfered with the employer's right to select its representative.

15. See, for example, *Kitsap County v. Kitsap County Juvenile Detention Officers' Guild*, Decision 12163 (PECB, 2014) (Washington state), where it was held "the employer's representatives at the table were not adequately informed, could not enter into tentative agreements (TAs) without consulting with those not at the bargaining table, could not adequately explain the employer's intent and unilaterally terminated bargaining," p. 1. Thus, the employer's representative at the table was "effectively hamstrung."

16. Roger Fisher and William Ury, *Getting to Yes: Negotiating Agreement without Giving In* (New York: Penguin Books, 1981), 148.

17. Permission to use "An Elegant Solution for the Negotiated Agreement" was granted by its author Richard Fossey, professor, University of North Texas, Denton, Texas, on January 3, 2009, via e-mail.

18. The argument from site administrators is that they do not want to be at the table because it may pit them against their teachers. School leaders will confront teachers who disagree with the position of the school district. Supporting the position of the school board/superintendent is part of the job of being a member of the leadership team. There is little difference for a school administrator to support the position of the school district at the bargaining table, at the school site, or in public. Argue in private, but support in public is a good refrain for school administrators. Ruben L. Ingram lists fifteen ways to involve principals in negotiations, "Negotiating Away Barriers to Educational Opportunity" *Leadership* 33 (2004): 28–31, 37–38, 29.

19. Todd A. DeMitchell, *Labor Relations in Education: Policies, Politics, and Practices* (Lanham, MD: Rowman & Littlefield Education, 2010), 118–19.

20. The comparison consists of fifteen diametrically opposed statements that differentiate dialogue from debate that were adapted to studying collective bargaining. For a listing of Sheldon Berman's comparison dialogue and debate items, see http://www.globallearningnj.org/global_ata/a_comparison_of_dialogue_and_debate.htm.

21. Michael R. Jette (2005), *Exploring Table Talk: Does Dialogue or Debate Correspond to Success and Satisfaction in Teacher Collective Bargaining?* Unpublished doctoral dissertation, University of New Hampshire, Durham, New Hampshire, p. 119. The debate/dialogue statements used in the research are found on pages 118 and 119.

22. Ibid., 87.

23. Ibid., 91.

24. Todd A. DeMitchell and Richard Barton, "Collective Bargaining and Its Impact on Local Educational Reform Efforts." *Educational Policy* 10 (1996): 366–78, 372.

Chapter 5

Conclusion

Ready to Bargain

Moving from a unionism built around diffidence and antagonism to one
built around cooperation requires mutual respect.[1]

Negotiating a good, sound contract is hard work. It takes patience, diligence, and
organization. Problem-solving skills, communication skills, the ability to look
someone in the eye and say no and then provide a rationale for the position, and
an ability to gain trust and to give trust when earned are important qualities.

William Keene's suggestion from just over twenty years ago is still sound
in the second decade of the twenty-first century. He states that the focus at
the bargaining table must move from " 'How much can we get (union) or keep
(management/board)?' to 'How can we fairly (to students, staff, and community) and wisely use the resources available to us?' "[2]

It is important to thoroughly analyze the existing contract language before
bargaining new language. Very seldom is obsolete language deleted from a
contract. New language for new concerns is just tacked on. One contract has
a section about the fair use of the old hand-cranked mimeograph machines—
the old purple plague of decades ago. Contract sections should be reviewed
looking for problems and highlighting deadlines. Preparation for bargaining
involves an analysis of a CBA's contract language looking for the good, the
bad, and the ugly. Reading contracts with a critical eye is important in bargaining a contract, as well as managing a contract's implementation.

THE ROLE OF THE SCHOOL BOARD

The school board is the major constituency for management's bargaining team.
The school board has ultimate legal responsibility for the contract. The board

and the union are the signatories to the contract. Teachers and administrators while impacted by the contract are not the parties to the contract. Consequently, this provides a conundrum for management's bargaining team that does not exist for labor's team—what role should a school board play in negotiations?

In many school districts, school board members not only sit at the bargaining table, but some are also the chief spokespersons. While many hold that school board members should not sit at the table, many believe the opposite.[3] The National School Board Association offers the following advice to the board and its members asking whether participation will:

1. not interfere with the bargaining process;
2. treat all information and parameters as highly confidential;
3. not discuss any negotiating topic or position with a unit member or association staff member;
4. support the chief negotiator and the positions he or she takes at the table. Understand that it is a common tactic for the association to blame the chief negotiator when they do not like the board's position. ("If we could just get rid of John we could get a contract.");
5. understand that the union will try to "work" a board member, either to gain confidential information or a favorable vote on the board;
6. respect all board positions as the position of the board, no matter the vote or how the individual board member voted; and
7. not make side deals with the union.[4]

REVIEWING THE CONTRACT

A close reading of the existing contract is important for preparing for the next contract. Below are a few thoughts on specific sections of the contract from the viewpoint of management. However, they are also instructive from the union side of the table.

Not all contract sections are well written. A poorly written contract section can lead to problems of implementation and contract creep in which the contract continues to expand in directions that do not serve the interests of management. Preparation for bargaining should include a detailed review of all contract sections looking for ambiguity, poorly written language, contradictory language, and vague language. These are a few good, bad, and ugly concerns about contract language.

- Too often contract language allows for "two bites of the apple" in which a legal right granted in state and federal law is stated as a right in the contract, thus allowing two opportunities to seek relief. If a right is granted by statute, an inclusion of the right in the contract is superfluous. It gives the employee a grievable right, unless there is positive assurance stating that the section is not grievable and thus not subject to arbitration. The legal remedy for the right should be the avenue used to seek redress of the right. William Sharp also agrees that it is not good management practice to agree to include statutes in the contract.[5]

In addition, some contract sections allow employees to grieve alleged violations of board policy. As discussed previously, the grievance hat is a narrow hat in which only the contract fits under it. The grievance process should not be the general vehicle for all conflict resolution.

- Use positive assurance to bracket those sections that you do not want to be grieved or arbitrated. It is best to be very explicit when a contract section is not subject to the grievance process. For example, the following taken from a contract is a succinct statement giving positive assurance: "The transfer decision is not grievable." Clear language like this reduces the likelihood of misunderstanding and/or allowance of unintended consequence of grieving and arbitrating a topic not intended to be grieved or arbitrated.

Early Retirement Incentive

Bargaining an ongoing early retirement incentive into the contract requires management to offer more than it would have if it wants to target a specific time for an incentive. Early retirement incentives should only be bargained with the goal that the district not lose money, but make money within five years.

The early retirement proposal has to save money for the school district over a five-year period. It is best to upfront about this requirement in bargaining and that the proposal is an incentive for retiring earlier than expected rather than a benefit of employment. A copy of how to do a five-year cost analysis when preparing an early retirement proposal is included in chapter 3.

It is only advantageous to the school district to offer an incentive if it induces an employee to retire that year rather than waiting another year or two. The employee who is going to retire anyway gets a bonus, and the district has spent money with no additional return.

A second issue associated with ongoing retirement incentive plans is that they sometimes are capped as to the number of individuals who can access the benefit. This underscores the purpose of the section, which is a benefit and not an incentive. If early retirement is an incentive, you place a minimum number on who can access it but not a maximum number of teachers as long as the requirement that within five years the district will save money is met. Early retirement can be both a personnel incentive—making room for newer teachers—and a financial incentive—replacing higher paid teachers with lower paid teachers—for school districts.

The Board and Binding Arbitration

Many if not most grievance language goes from the informal to the formal with the immediate supervisor, step two with the superintendent, step three with the school board, and step four with the arbitrator who renders a binding decision compelling the school board to implement the decision. It is questionable whether the school board should be one of the steps in a binding arbitration process. Politically it places the board in the position of having their position publicly overturned. The school board is placed in one of those rare situations in which their decision will ultimately be advisory to the next and final level of the decision process. Second, it adds time to the process. It is recommended to leave the school board out of the steps of binding arbitration. However, it is appropriate and necessary that they have a role in the process in advisory arbitration.

Question an Assumed or Stated Foundation for Elements of the Contract

Be careful of language that has a questionable legal foundation. For example, a contract has a section titled HIV/AIDS Confidentiality, which states that "any infected member is encouraged to notify the Superintendent or principal." This establishes language with tacit pressure for an individual to disclose a condition, which is confidential. The more puzzling language follows: "The District shall not discriminate against the infected member without cause."

If there is cause, is it discrimination? Under what conditions would the school district discriminate against a person with HIV/AIDS? Can contract language take away protections found under section 504 of the Rehabilitation Act? The answer is no.

Why was this language even negotiated? On top of it the section states that any breach of confidentiality "is subject to legal action by the member and the Association." This appears to give the Association standing to sue, but for what harm to the Association? What if it is a member of the union who reveals the confidential information, has the Association been harmed? It is clear that the employee who had his or her confidentiality breached would be harmed.

Nuts and Bolts

Bargaining is hard work. It requires preparation, organization, deft interpersonal skills, integrity, a willingness to check your ego at the door, and a focus on the relationship that will exist after the bargaining has been completed. This section on nuts and bolts offers a few tips based on experience at the table bargaining a contract and away from the table implementing the contract.

- Be straightforward, do not misrepresent or hide the facts.
- Be calm, patient, and tolerant.
- Do not be afraid to say no, but be willing to back it up as to why you have said no. A bad yes is much worse than a clear no. You live with yes much longer.
- Do not believe that you have the corner on truth, there are always things to learn from others.
- Your good word is one of the things that you own, protect it and use it wisely. It is fragile and can be damaged easily.
- When you make a mistake at the table, given wrong information, take responsibility at the table. Saying "I made a mistake" protects your good word in that others will know that there is integrity behind it and a genuine desire to be accurate and fair. It is what you would want to hear from others.
- Do not give a last offer unless it is the last offer. You cannot have more than one last offer.
- Be flexible with strategy and options, but protect the interests you seek at the table.
- Trashing the other side of the table is not a winning strategy. The public comes to believe that the inept are trying to lead the callous and indifferent.
- At the public-sector bargaining table, you do not represent yourself, you represent the constituency who asked you to bargain for them.
- Be cognizant of the conflict of interests that exists and try to expand the community of interests that also exists. Conflict does not go away. Community must be worked for and earned.
- Seeking cooperation and collegiality is preferable to cooptation. It also lasts longer.

The process and outcome of bargaining has important consequences. Bargaining must be approached thoughtfully with a clear understanding of the interests that must be pursued at the table which acknowledging the conflict of interests inherent in bargaining, the community of interests must be the favored ground sought by both parties. As stated earlier, the measure of success of bargaining is not a signed agreement; it is a contract that works for all.

NOTES

1. Charles T. Kerchner and Krista D. Caufman, "Building the Airplane While It's Rolling Down the Runway." In Charles T. Kerchner and Julie E. Koppich, *A Union of*

Professionals: Labor Relations and Educational Reform (New York: Teachers College Press, 1993), 16.

2. William G. Keane, *Win Win or Else: Collective Bargaining in an Age of Public Discontent.* (Thousand Oaks, CA: Corwin Press, Inc., 1996), 11.

3. Nancy J. Hungerford and Mark C. Blom, *Collective Bargaining and the Negotiation Process: A Primer for School Board Negotiators*, National School Boards Association/National School Boards Association Council of Attorneys, School Law Seminar, New Orleans, LA (2014). Visited July 23, 2017, available at https://www.nsba.org/sites/default/files/reports/Collective%20Bargaining%20and%20the%20 Negotiation%20Process.pdf.

It is relatively common in K–12 bargaining to have board members be part of the official bargaining team, but it varies by jurisdiction and the preference of the board in any given year. The board should consider whether members have the time necessary to commit to bargaining, and whether the board's need to be kept apprised of bargaining can be satisfied through some other mechanism, such as frequent updates from the bargaining team. Also, any board member agreeing to be on the negotiating team should understand that he or she becomes an unstated "power figure" to whom the union will direct their attention. This can erode the authority of the chief negotiator, place the board member in some uncomfortable situations, and occasionally cause friction among the other board members. Ibid., 7.

4. Ibid., 11.

5. William L. Sharp, *Winning at Collective Bargaining: Strategies Everyone can Live with.* (Lanham, MD: The Scarecrow Press, Inc., 2003), 78.

Section II

THE SIMULATION

Chapter 6

The Arroyo Wells School District Simulation

The following updated simulation, the AWSD Collective Bargaining Simulation, is the driving force in my collective bargaining class. The class is divided into two teams: management (AWSD—District) and labor (Arroyo Wells Teachers Association—AWTA). If the class is large, separate tables can be constructed and debriefing discussions can be used to discuss the differences that emerged at the multiple tables.

The teams start the first meeting getting to know each other and start to fashion a team response and not individual responses to the simulation. One part of the class sessions can be devoted to the academics of labor relations found in the companion volume (*Teachers and Their Unions: Labor Relations in Uncertain Times*) or in another labor relations book. The other part of the class is reserved for the students to work with their team to prepare for bargaining. The two teams prepare for bargaining throughout the semester. The teams receive the simulation and their interest letter from their constituency (Appendix A and Appendix B).

The instructor should play the role of the constituency for each team—the union president for AWTA (TAD) and the superintendent for the district (Dr. Oz). Bargaining teams, as discussed previously, do not represent their personal views, interests, and needs. They represent the interests and needs of the constituency they represent at the table. The instructor serving as the constituency for both parties allows her/him to work with both teams clarifying questions and providing for each sides bargaining strategies.

The bargaining is expedited. Ten hours (two five-hour sessions) at the end of the semester is reserved for bargaining. No other class activities take place during bargaining. If the teams wish to meet ahead of time to discuss ground rules or to share their bargaining "interests," I allow time for those discussions. They can communicate separate from class via meetings or electronically. Their constituency should always be apprised of such communications.

73

This is consistent with the propositions that bargaining teams represent their constituency and that bargaining teams also bargain with their constituency.

When the bargaining begins, videotaping the sessions for analysis at the end of the bargaining class is a useful strategy. Debriefing on what worked well and what could have worked better is a useful strategy. A comparison of the interest letter for each side helps to ascertain if the interests were successfully pursued by each side.

The teams work out their own table process/ground rules for bargaining. They call their caucuses and resume when they are ready. They decide whether there will be a chief spokesperson or whether their table talk is ad hoc with all participating, or whether they assign specific issues to individuals.

The instructor can sit in on caucuses and can also respond to questions from the teams as either their union president or superintendent when they are trying out proposals that meet their interests and creatively try to meet the interests of the other party.

Most classes, but not all, settle the contract. However, as discussed earlier, the measure of success of bargaining is not in signing an agreement. The measure of success is the extent to which relations are improved or harmed. Bargaining that is considered problem-solving is more effective. In the converse, bargaining that results in a contract, but just adds to the baggage of bad feelings and sets the stage for more animosity and a belief that my victory is only achieved at vanquishing you.

For each side, a letter of interest that should guide each sides' bargaining is found in the appendices: the union's letter is given in appendix A and management's letter is given in appendix B. Appendix C is a letter that can be sent prior to bargaining. The appendices and the Flash News Updates are intended to keep the bargaining as real as possible. Each member of the simulation must only read their letter of interest depending on the team they are representing. In addition a sample debriefing format and news flashes are included.

THE SIMULATION

AWSD is a public school district. It is a kindergarten through twelfth-grade district with four elementary schools (K–5), one middle school (6–8), one high school (9–12). There are 2,800 students with 175 certificated faculty members not counting classified staff and administrative staff. The faculty is older with a mean age of forty-seven.

The town of Arroyo Wells is semirural. The farms and expanses of woods are giving way to development. The population has been slowly growing with mainly younger professionals and semi-professionals moving in as a means to escape from the metropolitan area. Many of these new families have toddlers or are just starting a family. This shift in population will cause a population bubble to run through the school in the next three to five years. Aside from these newcomers, there is a long-term population that has maintained the power base and they are happy with the way things are and have always been.

The school district enjoys a deserved reputation for excellence. It attracts quality teachers who stay once they have been hired. Few teachers see Arroyo Wells as a way station as they look for better positions. The district has lower class sizes than many other surrounding school districts and its salary schedule is considered to be quite good. This is a source of pride for residents, parents, and the school district's employees. The schools consistently score at or near the top in state tests.

The town has a population of around 17,000 full-time residents. It is located about thirty miles from one of the state's population centers that provides employment for most of the newcomers and some of the established residents. The State University is approximately fifteen miles away and provides education opportunities for the faculty.

The socioeconomic status of the school district is strong. This is in part because the town is considered an attractive place to live with good schools, easy communicate to employment opportunities, and proximity of very good state university. The Aid for Dependent Children (AFDC) percentage for Arroyo Wells is 7 percent. This compares favorably to the two local school districts, which both the union and management consider to be comparators. Metroville School District has an AFDC percentage of 26 and Happy Valley School District has an AFDC percentage of 15.

The cost of living for the past three years has been 3.50 percent, 3.45 percent, and 3.00 percent. The current cost of living is 3.70 and is projected to be steady throughout the year. The town employees in Arroyo Wells have received the following raises during the past three years: last year—3.25 percent, year before—3.0 percent, and three years ago—2.50 percent (see data section for comparative pay raises with Metroville School District and Happy Valley School District). The town employees have been perceived as being paid less than the teachers and to have been treated less fairly than the teachers when it comes to salary.

The last contract was finally negotiated with both the superintendent and union president participating in the process. It was a three-year zippered contract with pay raises built in but with no financial escape clause. The contract is expiring. The raises for the three previous years were 3.50 percent, 3.0 percent, and 2.75 percent. Funding from the State is relatively flat and the local population is concerned about rising property taxes. Many of the older residents want the school district to hold the line on expenditures, believing that the teachers are overpaid for their "part-time" jobs. However, the newer residents strongly support the schools and the school district. Real estate agents support the schools and routinely point to the schools as a sell-ing point. Consequently, housing prices have risen and developers seek to build in the community.

The high salary and the low class size have combined to strain the financial resources of the school district. The district believes, and is not refuted by the AWTA, that both of these issues have required that during the past two years the district has had to use funds from its reserve and to delay needed preventive maintenance work on the schools in order to balance the budget. (See Demographics at the end of the chapter.)

THE DISTRICT AND AWTA NEGOTIATIONS

Negotiations have been going on for several months with little progress. Both sides have decided to try two days of expedited negotiating sessions in order to try to bring in contract, if possible. If these sessions fail, both sides will mutually declare impasse and request a mediator as per state law. Tentative agreement had already been reached on all of the easy items. The difficult items remain. Listed below are the unresolved issues and each side's last position. The last offer from the school district accompanies each unresolved section.

Note that where a contract section states "No Change" it means that the current language has been accepted by both sides and need not be negotiated. Back-up data are provided at the end of the chapter.

Each side will develop proposals on each of the following unresolved issues. They can use supposals and water cooler negotiations to augment the proposals. In addition, I issue a few News Flashes that will occur in the readings that may impact bargaining. I have placed the News Flashes at the end of the chapter. They can be used at any point in the simulation. I issue the first News Flash before the start of negotiations and the second the night before negotiations.

Salary

The district ended the past two years with reserves of less than 5 percent. It had some unexpected maintenance issues that overwhelmed its small, deferred maintenance budget. In addition, it hired some new teachers because of some increased class sizes. The district received criticism from some of the established community members about paying high salaries with low class sizes thus placing a burden on the taxpayer. The superintendent and Board of Trustees are sensitive to comments about "loose" spending and want to hold the line with this round of bargaining.

In addition, the escalating costs of fringe benefits are placing a strain on the budget. This is especially true since the district currently pays 100 percent of the cost for medical, dental, life, and disability insurance. The district cannot sustain this practice.

Each 1 percent increase on the salary schedule costs approximately $160,000 in salary and corresponding fixed fringe benefits costs such as retirement, social security, and insurances.

AWTA: The union came down from its original position of 8 percent to its last proposal of 5 percent. The union also is resistant to the proposed language (see later) on remediation plans and movement on the salary schedule. It is somewhat open to a vertical freeze as long as the unit member is restored to the place where they would have been had they not been frozen. It is opposed to a horizontal freeze arguing that the graduate credits have been earned separate from the teaching of the unit member. It has not offered a response to the early retirement portion of the new language.

DISTRICT: Management has maintained a 1 percent increase from the beginning of bargaining to its last offer. It has argued that any increase in the ongoing expenditures, such as increases to the salary schedule, needs to be offset with cost decreases such as decreases to the fringe benefit costs through burden-sharing. But, it also knows that it will need to increase the offer, especially if it wants to do retrieval bargaining by having the union move from the district paying 100 percent of fringe benefit costs.

In addition, management seeks to add the following statement to the salary schedule: "Unit members who are currently on a Remediation Plan cannot move laterally or horizontally on the salary schedule. Similarly, they cannot receive a longevity stipend. Once the unit member has been removed from the Remediation Plan the Unit Member can continue to follow the schedule. Any lost vertical movement cannot be restored. Additionally, a unit member cannot take part in any early retirement plan if he or she is on a Remediation Plan."

This new language is sought because a unit member was on the second year of a remediation plan and received vertical and horizontal movement. The public found out about it and raised concerns during budget deliberations. Management consider this unacceptable and against the concept of recognizing only success in teaching.

Fringe Benefits

For the current year, AWSD's medical insurance rates rose 8.6 percent. Over the past ten-year period, the medical insurance rates rose an average of

12 percent. Last year the rates only rose 2 percent. Dental insurance has followed a similar pattern with a slightly smaller rise in premiums—3 percent this year. Arroyo Wells is the only school district in the surrounding area that pays 100 percent of the medical and dental insurances. Arroyo Wells and the two comparator school districts, Metroville School District and Happy Valley School District, pay for life insurance and disability insurance.

AWTA: The union wants to keep the current 100 percent district-paid benefits. However, it knows that it is not realistic. The increased costs of fringe benefits erode the amount of new revenue available for salary. The older teachers want a higher salary so that their retirement will increase. They are less concerned with fringe benefits since their children have grown and left home or they do not have children. The younger teachers, especially those with families, want a high salary also, but voice a need for good medical and dental benefits for their family.

DISTRICT: The district has a strong interest in shifting some of the burden of increased fringe benefit costs to the employee. As a show of good faith, the district, through the superintendent, has informed the management team that the district would no longer pay 100 percent of the costs for fringe benefits. They are discussing whether to place a dollar cap on the amount of fringe benefits that the district would pay or whether to move to a percentage that the district pays for insurance. The two surrounding comparator school districts have burden-sharing in their contract. Metroville School District has a 85/15 percent split in which the school district pays 85 percent of medical and dental and the employee pays 15 percent. The percentages stay the same as the cost of insurance rises.

Happy Valley has a dollar amount cap. The cap is for a maximum monthly dollar amount. At this point the dollar cap covers the cost of single coverage for all insurances. However, the cap does not cover all of the costs for the most expensive medical insurance for family. Happy Valley pays $1,500 a month for medical and dental insurance. This covers the most expensive costs for a single subscriber ($31.58 for dental and $552.59 for medical = $584.17) but does not cover the costs for family ($109.12 for dental and $1,492.00 for medical = $1,601.12). Unit members who cover family in these two plans would pay out-of-pocket $101.12 per month. However, if the school district has other insurance options that are less costly, the employee has the option of moving to a lower cost insurance plan during the open enrollment period. A dollar cap forces the Association to negotiate a larger dollar amount for the cap. The district argues that would allow the Association to make reasoned choices between how it wants to distribute limited resources available for salary and fringe benefits to its membership.

Extra Duty Salary Schedule

The extra duty salary schedule is based on a formula with a unit value of $310 applied to a sliding scale of units based on the time commitment and the level of supervision. For example, the athletic director has a unit value of 4.25 and the middle school yearbook advisor has a unit value of 1.75.

AWTA: The union has proposed that the dollar amount be changed to a percentage of the beginning salary, Step 1 Column A. Its last offer was 1.5 percent of the beginning salary.

DISTRICT: The district has rejected the offer stating that it would constitute an increased cost each year if the beginning salary was increased. Its last position was "no change" to the current contract.

Class Size

AWTA: The union has proposed a class size reduction of one student in all categories (see end of chapter contract sections). It asserts that smaller class sizes are necessary for students if they are to meet state standards. The union points out that parents strongly support small class size.

DISTRICT: The district has proposed an increase in class size of one student for each category. The district asserts that there is no research evidence that reducing class size by one student, given the current class size language, significantly improves student learning. And conversely, they argue that there is no research that supports that an increase of one student will significantly harm student learning. The district views this as not only an educational issue but a financial issue as well. A reduction of class size will necessitate the hiring of more teachers. An increase in class size will slow the hiring of teachers and thus the pressure on the budget.

Leaves

8.6   Adoption and Child-Rearing Leave
A member of the unit (male or female) who wishes to take a personal leave to raise a child immediately following childbirth or upon adoption of a child may be granted such leave without pay for up to one (1) year.

AWTA: The union wants the leave to be with half pay as if it were a sabbatical. Their argument is that it is the right thing to do.

DISTRICT: The district states that it is a cost item in a time when the budget is a concern. If AWTA wants this cost item what is it willing to give up in order to get it? In addition, the district argues that personal leave to raise a child is not like a sabbatical that involves extended study, which benefits the district and its students.

Reassignment within a School

Language in pertinent part reads:

ARTICLE 10 TRANSFER PROCEDURE

10.3   Involuntary Transfer

10.31 The District shall seek volunteers prior to making any involuntary transfer/reassignment. If an involuntary transfer/reassignment becomes necessary, the unit member with the least District seniority shall be transferred or reassigned.

Background: Application of 10.31

In order to reassign one history teacher (#1) at the middle school from five periods of eighth-grade history to four periods of eighth-grade history and one period of seventh-grade history and there were no volunteers the following would occur. A teacher (#2) at the high school would have to be reassigned for one period to the middle school. A history teacher (#3) at the high school would be reassigned to the one period that missing period of history at the high school level. The course that that teacher was reassigned came from his physical education assignment. The next least senior teacher (#4) to fill that physical education class has an English credential and is pulled from the English curriculum. The next least senior teacher (#5) who holds a credential in English is at the middle school. That teacher is assigned one period of physical education at the high school. The seventh-grade English class, which now must be staffed comes from the journalism program. That teacher (#6) is pulled from a journalism class. The other journalism teacher who also holds a credential in English (#7) must now pick up one additional period of journalism, thus creating an opening. This teacher does not like teaching the low-level seventh-grade English class and thus does not volunteer. This still creates an opening for an English class which the original teacher who started the fall of the dominos (#1) cannot teach because he does not possess the appropriate credential and is still without his fifth teaching assignment. To fill the English position, a special education teacher (#8) who has dual certification is pulled from his special education class. The next least senior special education teacher teaches at Central Elementary School. Her position at Central is now filled by a third-grade teacher (#9) who recently returned to the regular classroom. Teacher

(#1) still does not have a position. We have two special education classes in which the teacher must leave for one period a day to cover classes. The bumping can still continue because teacher (#1) does not have an assignment and all other history teachers are very high on the seniority list.

A similar scenario can be played out at the elementary school if a teacher who teaches third grade one year is reassigned to second grade the next year because of a change in student enrollment.

AWTA: The Association stated that they might be willing to trade language changes in the current contract for some acceptable rewording of section 10.31. The Director of Personnel stated that the district would not be leveraged into opening up a zippered contract and that the district might force the issue into arbitration. The Director also stated the feeling of the management team that AWTA was not dealing in a fair manner and that AWTA was just opportunistic which does not breed harmonious labor relations. The issue was still not resolved at the time that negotiations started for the new contract. There were no pending grievances on section 10.31 although there were occasional grumbles and threats when some individuals were upset with decisions made by the administration.

DISTRICT: Several months following the ratification of the contract, the principal of the middle school discussed plans with his staff for the following year's teaching assignments. As in the past, a number of the teachers' assignments would be altered to meet changing student needs. In the past the principal had always had the discretion to make reasonable changes within the confines of an individual's teaching credential. These changes were not considered a violation of the contract but instead a part of doing business. This changed that spring; two teachers at the school did not like the planned changes and complained strenuously to the principal, AWTA, and the lounge, in general. The two teachers eventually filed a grievance citing the new language in section 10.31. The teachers contended that the administration could not involuntarily "reassign" them from their present assignment. If a reassignment was necessary the district had to move the least senior district employee. The administration objected vehemently to this interpretation. AWTA backed the two teachers publicly but privately some of the AWTA negotiators stated that that interpretation was never intended. The administration backed down from the intended change at that time, but registered a complaint with AWTA and requested a discussion session to iron out the situation.

The meeting in September of last year did not go well. AWTA contended that they intended the language of that section to apply to any reassignment, even a change from teaching seventh-grade history one year to teaching eighth-grade history the following year. The district contended that they never would have agreed to such ridiculously confining language had they known the union's interpretation. AWTA countered that the district could use the seniority of the school to implement the language of section 10.31. The district responded that that construction was never advanced by the union and thus, was never intended to be part of it. In addition, the only accepted definition in the contract and through past practice was that seniority was district seniority, the point that the employee started to work for the district. The district does not even keep records specific to how long an employee has been employed at a specific school. It has flatly rejected the idea of altering the concept of seniority from district seniority to school seniority.

The district wants the word reassignment removed from section 10.31.

PROFESSIONAL ASSIGNMENTS—ARTICLE 7

7.7 ACTIVITIES/ASSIGNMENTS

Members of the unit shall participate in professional activities and perform professional assignments beyond the regular workday as needed and consistent with past practices of the District.

AWTA: The union has put forward language to remove this section of the contract in each of the past three contracts. Each time they withdrew their proposal to gain other concessions and to get a contract. Over the past five years there have been five grievances filed regarding this section. Each grievance tried to demonstrate that a particular management practice was in violation of this article. Part of their argument was cast along the lines that this language was too vague to be implemented. Four of those grievances originated at the high school and one at the middle school. All five were closely linked in time to upcoming contract negotiations. The grievances typically centered on after-school committee work, parent-teacher conferences, and after-school duties. One of the grievances, actually filed under section 7.3, was taken to advisory arbitration. Section 7.3 was used to try to get around the singular lack of union success with section 7.7. The arbitrator upheld the grievance but the board rejected it based on the past practice of section 7.7.

DISTRICT: There is no definition of section 7.7. It typically has been used to mean that teachers had to attend committee meetings and to meet with parents or administrators. It is invoked very rarely by administration as a rationale for its decisions. Past practice is on the side of management in that when section 7.7 has been used its application has been somewhat of an expansive incorporating several different types of activities. The other key to this issue is that AWTA has given up its position with regard to section 7.7 in the past in order to secure a contract. AWTA's desire to remove section 7.7 has never formed the basis for impasse in prior negotiations.

The district has consistently refused to remove or change the language. In fact, at several times of frustration at the bargaining table, the district negotiators have remarked that it is the only place where the term professional appears in the contract.

GRIEVANCES—ARBITRATION—ARTICLE 6

In the past ten years only four grievances have been heard and decided by an arbitrator. In three of the cases the Board accepted the decision of the arbitrator; one of those decisions went against the district. The Board rejected one decision. The issue centered around sections 7.3 and 7.7. AWTA argued that mandatory department committee meetings at the high school violated section 7.3. The arbitrator agreed. The Board agreed with management that the applicable section was 7.7 and it was controlling because of the long past practice of mandatory departmental meetings.

AWTA: The Association wants binding arbitration, arguing that it was a fair and accepted practice.

DISTRICT: The school board has consistently argued that they were elected by the community and that it would be a dereliction of their duty to turn over decision-making to a third party via binding arbitration.

EVALUATION—ARTICLE 12

12.12 Procedure
   (a) Every probationary member of the unit shall be evaluated in writing by his/her immediate supervisor/principal in writing at least no later than February 15.
   (b) Any member of the unit who receives a negative evaluation shall, upon request, be entitled to two (2) subsequent observations and a written evaluation of the observations. If the deficiency(ies) noted in the negative have been corrected, the second evaluation shall become part of the unit member's file, and shall be attached to the original evaluation.
   (e) The evaluation of members of the unit, except for alleged violation of procedural matters, shall not be subject to the Grievance Procedure.

AWTA: The union is willing to trade the language that the district wants for section 12.12(a) for what it wants for section 12.12(e). However, it is concerned that moving the deadline closer to the mandated state law deadline will negatively impact section 12.12(b) which provides for two additional observations following a negative evaluation.

DISTRICT: The district believes that the February 15 deadline for a written evaluation comes too soon. The state deadline for renominating probationary teachers is April 15. The administrators want to have an extra month and one-half, to the first of April, for the last written evaluation. They argue that the additional time may make the difference in a positive or negative employment decision. This change, the administration's bargaining team asserts, is in the best interests of the teacher.

AWTA: The Association wants to grieve the content of the evaluation, not just the procedures used in the evaluation. The union believes that its members need to be protected from incompetent or vindictive administrators. The ability to grieve the content of an evaluation, the union negotiating team asserts, keeps the evaluation honest.

DISTRICT: Management is emphatic in saying no. They believe that it would clearly erode their ability to supervise the faculty. They also assert that an arbitrator may not be an educator and would thus not understand the pedagogy and research that supports evaluations. Consequently, the arbitrator would likely be confined to those elements of labor relations that they understand, such as the procedural aspects of the evaluation which is already protected.

SICK LEAVE SEPARATION—ARTICLE 14

The issue of overuse of sick leave has recently surfaced again. There was an increase in the percentage of unit members who used 100 percent of their sick leave. Two contracts ago a sick leave separation benefit was bargained into the contract. The use of sick leave was reduced, but it has risen this year as both sides agreed on the statistics. The union recommends that the section benefits be improved to induce a more judicious use of sick leave while the school district is looking at making it harder to use sick leave by requiring a note from a physician. Neither side has presented a formal written proposal. Instead they have engaged in conversations about the contract section and offered supposals to the conversation. It was left with the statement that either side can bring this section into the expedited bargaining if they wish.

AWTA: The union is interested in increasing the percentage of reimbursement from 35 percent of the members per diem to 50 percent of the members per diem. The union has also discussed increasing the maximum of accumulated sick leave from 120 days to 150 days.

DISTRICT: The district is considering shortening the time frame for section moving from six years to ten years. Management has not offered any increase from 35 percent nor has it offered to increase the number of accumulated days. Their chief spokesperson also discussed linking it to retirement or to a minimum age of fifty-five years tying it to a retirement benefit.

Early Retirement Incentive

Of the two neighboring school districts, only Happy Valley gave any type of an early retirement incentive plan. The plan was offered during the past school year for one time only. The district offered to pay the medical and dental benefits for the employee and his or her spouse up to the maximum cap allowable under the current contract (whatever cap is in the contract each year) to age sixty-five. The employee must have worked in the district for at least ten years and be at least fifty-five years of age during the year that he or she retires. Previously, the employee could purchase the insurance at the group rate.

The last CBA had a one-time only early retirement plan. The cost of the Supplemental Early Retirement Plan (SERP) was approximately 20,000 per retiree (it varied according to the employee's salary and years worked in the state) paid out over five years to the contracting company. Six people took advantage of the SERP. All retiree positions were filled. The amount of savings is unknown.

AWTA: The leadership wants an early retirement incentive package. There are a large number (thirty-six) of staff members who are at least fifty-five years old. This is a powerful group of teachers. AWTA also asserts that an incentive that assists highly paid teachers to retire will result in a savings to the district when it hires lower paid teachers. The union wants a multiyear incentive arguing that teachers deserve the incentive and should have flexibility in deciding when to accept the incentive and retire.

DISTRICT: The district is not against this proposal per se but holds that any early retirement incentive must improve the district's financial condition within five years. In other words, the district has stated that within five years the cost of the incentive must be outweighed by the savings generated by the incentive. The district only wants a one-year incentive arguing that the incentive must be an inducement for teachers to retire earlier than they would have. The district does not save money by giving an incentive to someone who had intended to retire anyway, it argues.

Debriefing

By videotaping of the bargaining, water cooler negotiations, and the occasional caucus, selections can be selected by the instructor for viewing and discussion. The following is the debriefing memo that can be sent to the class prior to the debriefing to provide a format.

DEBRIEFING

1. What surprised you at the table?
2. Were you prepared enough for bargaining? Was the other side prepared enough?
3. What were your takeaways from the simulation, what did you learn?
4. How did the use of technology influence, facilitate, or inhibit bargaining? What aspects worked the best? Once language was discussed at the table (supposals) and was typed into the applicable contract section and then appeared on the screen, was there a sense that the language had been agreed upon because it appeared on screen? Were you reluctant to change or challenge it once it was written for all to see?
5. Compare your contract with the Interest Letter that you received from your constituency. Did you meet or violate the interests? Management expanded leaves, why?
6. What was your discussion like on the topic of putting the most difficult money sections first?
7. Did you caucus too much, too little, or just right?
8. Was water cooler negotiations a successful strategy?
9. How different was the second session of bargaining from the first? Why?
10. What role did personality play at the table?
11. Did you keep your constituency informed?
12. Did you find that you bargained with the other two parties, your team, and your constituency?
13. Did you bring the principles of *Getting Together* and *Getting to Yes* to the table?

NEWS FLASHES

INSTRUCTOR: Please use these News Flashes at two selected points of your choosing in the simulation. They should stimulate discussion and response.

News Flash #1

NEWS FLASH••NEWS FLASH••NEWS FLASH

The Rio Grande Condo project has just opened and a number of families with school age children have moved into the condos. It is estimated that the new condos and other planned projects in the school district will result in a generation factor of 0.32 students over the next five to seven years yielding a net of fifty to seventy students. The new students in the last two weeks of the opening of the project have impacted the class sizes at Mesquite Elementary School in several of the elementary schools as have the arrival of several new families at Center School and Sierra Vista Elementary School. The middle school and the high school class sizes have been unaffected. There have been some grumbles about filing grievances but none have been filed as of yet. At least eight classes are now at maximum size.

Listed below are the schools and classes that now exceed the contractual limit of 9.1.

Mesquite Elementary School
One Kindergarten—twenty-five students
One First Grade—twenty-six students
Center School
One First Grade—twenty-six students

There is little migration during the school year. The elementary schools average about a turnover rate of 0.20. In other words, if you have a school with 100 students during the course of the school year, approximately 120 students will enroll in the school throughout the school year.

News Flash #2

NEWS FLASH••NEWS FLASH••NEWS FLASH

It was just reported that Metroville School District settled their contract. The teachers will receive a 2 percent increase plus $250 for each placement on the salary schedule for the first year (the $250 is off the salary schedule and is a one-time payment), a 2.5 percent increase for the second year, and a 2.5 percent increase for the third year of the contract. The split of 85/15 for medical benefits remains unchanged. Fifteen minutes was added to the workday to accommodate the fifteen minutes added to the student schedule.

88

Chapter 6

CONTRACT SECTIONS

The contract sections below reflect the state of bargaining as you prepare for expedited bargaining. The language is the current language. Where "No Change" is indicated, it means that the proposals for both the district and the union match with neither seeking a change in the language. All other language is open for negotiations.

ARTICLE 6

Grievance Procedure
(The Informal and Level 1 stages of the Grievance Procedure are not contested.)

6.0   No Change
6.1   No Change
6.2   No Change
6.3   No Change
6.31 No Change
6.32 No Change
6.33 No Change
6.34 Level 2 Superintendent
      If the aggrieved person is not satisfied with the disposition of his grievance at Level 1, or if no decision has been rendered within five (5) school days after the presentation of the grievance, he/she may file the grievance in writing within five (5) school days after the decision at Level 1 or ten (10) school days after the grievance was presented, whichever is sooner, to the Superintendent with the objective of resolving the matter.
6.35 Level 3 Advisory Arbitration
      (a) If the aggrieved person is not satisfied with the disposition of the grievance at Level 2, or if no decision has been rendered within ten (10) school days after the grievance was delivered to the Superintendent, she/he may, within five (5) school days after the decision by the Superintendent or fifteen (15) school days after the grievance was delivered to the Superintendent, whichever is sooner, request in writing that the grievance be submitted to advisory arbitration. The Association shall retain the right to determine whether a grievance may proceed to arbitration.

(b) Within ten (10) school days after such written notice of submission to advisory arbitration, the Board and the Association shall attempt to agree upon a mutually acceptable arbitrator and shall obtain a commitment from said arbitrator to serve. If the parties are unable to agree upon an arbitrator or to obtain such a commitment within the specified time, a request may be made to the American Arbitration Association (AAA) by either party. The parties shall then be bound by the rules and procedures of the AAA in the selection of an arbitrator.

(c) The arbitrator so selected shall confer with the representatives of the Board and the Association and hold hearings promptly and shall issue an award not later than twenty (20) days from date of the close of the hearings or, if oral hearings have been waived by both parties, then from the date of the submission of final statements and proofs. The arbitrator's recommendation shall set forth his/her findings of fact, reasoning, and conclusions on the issue(s) submitted.

6.36 Level 4
The award of the arbitrator shall be final unless overturned by the Board within thirty (30) days of the rendering of the award. The decision of the Board shall be final and binding on the school district.

6.4 Rights of Teachers to Representation
Any aggrieved person may be represented at all stages of the grievance procedure by herself/himself, or, at her/his option, be accompanied by a representative of the Association.

6.5 Rights of Participants
No reprisals of any kind shall be taken by the Board or by any member of the administration against any party in interest, any representative, any member of the Association, or any participants in a grievance by reason of such participation.

ARTICLE 7

Hours of Employment

7.1 No Change
7.2 No Change
7.3 Meetings

Faculty meetings shall not exceed fifteen (15) per year, as needed and shall not exceed one (1) hour in duration, except in cases of emergency. Emergency is defined to mean a sudden unexpected happening, or an unforeseen event or condition, or a sudden or unexpected occasion for action and is beyond the control of the District.

7.4 No Change

7.5 No Change

7.6 Required Participation

Each member of the unit shall participate in the required Back-To-School and Open House nights, as well as participate in three (3) adjunct duties or ten (10) hours of adjunct duty (whichever comes first) related to student activities per year.

Examples of duties related to Student Activities are athletic events, club activities, dances, music, and drama events, and other social events. These adjunct duties shall be scheduled equitably among the members of the unit at each school site.

7.7 Activities/Assignments

Members of the unit shall participate in professional activities and perform professional assignments beyond the regular workday as needed and consistent with past practices of the District.

ARTICLE 8

Leaves

8.1 No Change

8.2 No Change

8.3 No Change

8.4 No Change

8.5 No Change

8.6 Adoption & Child-Rearing Leave

A member of the unit (male or female) who wishes to take a personal leave to raise a child immediately following childbirth or upon adoption of a child may be granted such leave without pay for up to one (1) year.

ARTICLE 9

Class Size

9.1   General

The following class sizes shall be defined as applicable for all schools in the District.

Grades: K   24
Grades 1–3   25
Grades 4–5   27
Grades 6–12   29 with the exception of science laboratories which shall have a maximum of 24 students.

9.2   Combination Classes
The class size for elementary classes, which combine one or more grade levels shall be reduced by two. The lower class size shall be used as the base for the reduction in class size.

9.3   Preparation time for middle and high school—No Change

9.4   300 Minutes of Preparation time every ten work days—No Change

9.5   Student class assignments shall be made by the principal, or his her designee. If student class assignments have been made by what would go over the class size limits stated in 9.1, the principal, or designee, shall follow the procedures below:

9.51   Combining Classes
Combination classes should be established by the principal if this procedure will bring the affected class(es) within the applicable maximum.

9.52   School Reassignment
The District administration may reassign students to other schools in the District is such a reassignment would bring the affected class(es) within the applicable maximum.

9.53   Other
When class sizes are exceeded or none of the procedures of 9.61 and 9.62 are feasible, the principal shall discuss the problem with the teachers of the affected classes and explore alternative approaches to resolve the problem.

ARTICLE 10

Transfer Procedure

10.1   Primary Consideration
The primary consideration in affecting assignments and transfers shall be to provide the best possible educational program for students and to assure that the needs of the school system will best be met.

10.2   General Principles

10.21 Transfer
A transfer is the movement of a unit member from one work location to another work location at a different work site.

10.22 Reassignment
A reassignment is the movement of a unit member from one subject area or grade level to another grade level at the same work site.

10.23 Bias
A transfer/reassignment shall not be made or denied arbitrarily, capriciously, or without a basis in fact.

10.3   Involuntary Transfer

10.31 The District shall seek volunteers prior to making any involuntary transfer/reassignment. If an involuntary transfer/reassignment becomes necessary, the unit member with the least District seniority shall be transferred or reassigned.

ARTICLE 12

Evaluation

12.1   Purpose
It is agreed and understood by the parties that the principal objective of the performance evaluation procedure is to maintain or improve the quality of education in the District.

12.12 Procedure
(a) Every probationary member of the unit shall be evaluated in writing by his/her immediate supervisor/principal in writing at least no later than February 15.

(b) Any member of the unit who receives a negative evaluation shall, upon request, be entitled to two (2) subsequent observations and a written evaluation of the observations. If the deficiency(ies) noted in the negative have been corrected, the second evaluation shall become part of the unit member's file, and shall be attached to the original evaluation.

(c) Hearsay shall not be included in a unit member's evaluation.

(d) A member of the unit shall have the right to have appended to an evaluation his/her response to the evaluation within twenty (20) school days of receipt of the evaluation. Such appended responses shall become part of the employee's personnel file. In all cases, the unit member shall be provided with copies of and all of her/his evaluations.

(e) The evaluation of members of the unit, except for alleged violation of procedural matters, shall not be subject to the Grievance Procedure.

12.2 Evaluation and Personnel Records
All materials, documents, and evidence used to form the evaluation/discipline of a unit member shall be open to inspection by the unit member. The unit member shall be notified in a timely fashion when materials, documents, evidence are placed in the unit member's personnel file that could be used for evaluation/discipline. The unit member shall have the right to timely append comments to such placed material, documents, and evidence.

ARTICLE 14

Sick Leave Separation

1 The certificated teaching staff earns one day of sick leave per month up to 10 months per year (10 sick leave days per year maximum).

2 Each person may accumulate up to a maximum of 120 days of sick leave. Upon separation, after five consecutive years of service in the district, the certificated staff member shall be reimbursed for any earned but unused days of sick leave up to the maximum of 120 days at 35% of his/her per diem salary as per the existing salary schedule. The per diem is based on the contracted 183 days for teachers.

3 Extra-curricular, summer school, special extra-duty hourly wages, and/or special project payments shall not be computed in the per diem salary computation for reimbursement of unused sick leave days.

DEMOGRAPHICS

Table 6.1.   Certificated Staff Distribution.

Mesquite Elementary School	17 teachers
Center School	19 teachers
Sierra Vista Elementary School	15 teachers
Main Street School	18 teachers
Abenaqui Middle School	35 teachers
Arroyo Wells High School	42 teachers
Psychologists	4
Nurses	3
Music/Physical Education	8 for elementary schools
Special Education Teachers	14
Administrators	Superintendent
	Assistant superintendent for curriculum
	Director of personnel and labor relations
	Director of business services
	6 principals
	2 assistant principals

CLASS SIZES FOR THE SCHOOLS

Special education classes are not counted in these data.

Table 6.2.   Mesquite Elementary School (K–5), 405 Students.

Grade Level	No. of Students	Grade Level	No. of Students
Kindergarten	22	First	23
Kindergarten	24	First	23
Kindergarten	23	First	24
Grade Level	No. of Students	Grade Level	No. of Students
Second	22	Third	24
Second	24	Third	25
Second/Third	20	Third	24
Grade Level	No. of Students	Grade Level	No. of Students
Fourth	25	Fifth	26
Fourth	25	Fifth	25
Fourth	26		

Table 6.3.   Center School (K–5), 449 Students.

Grade Level	No. of Students	Grade Level	No. of Students
Kindergarten	23	First	23
Kindergarten	22	First	23

(Continued)

Table 6.3. Continued

Grade Level	No. of Students	Grade Level	No. of Students
Kindergarten	24	First	23
		First/Second	20
Grade Level	No. of Students	Grade Level	No. of Students
Second	24	Third	24
Second	22	Third	23
Second	23	Third	24
Grade Level	No. of Students	Grade Level	No. of Students
Fourth	25	Fifth	26
Fourth	25	Fifth	25
Fourth	26	Fifth	24

Table 6.4. Sierra Vista Elementary School (K–5), 350 Students.

Grade Level	No. of Students	Grade Level	No. of Students
Kindergarten	21	First	23
Kindergarten	21	First	22
Kindergarten	22	First	22
Grade Level	No. of Students	Grade Level	No. of Students
Second	23	Third	24
Second	23	Third	23
Second	23		
Grade Level	No. of Students	Grade Level	No. of Students
Fourth	25	Fifth	26
Fourth	26	Fifth	26

Table 6.5. Main Street School (K–5), 418 Students.

Grade Level	No. of Students	Grade Level	No. of Students
Kindergarten	22	First	23
Kindergarten	21	First	22
Kindergarten	22	First	23
Grade Level	No. of Students	Grade Level	No. of Students
Second	22	Third	22
Second	24	Third	23
Second	23	Third	23
Grade Level	No. of Students	Grade Level	No. of Students
Fourth	24	Fifth	26
Fourth	24	Fifth	25
Fourth	24	Fifth	25

Middle and High Enrollment

Abenaqui Middle School (6–8), 528 students
Arroyo Wells High School (9–12) 642 students

Table 6.6. Arroyo Wells School District.

Teacher Seniority List

Years of Service

Year	No. of Teachers	Year	No. of Teachers
2016–	1	1991–	6
2015	2	1990–	10
2014–	2	1989–	8
2013–	2	1988–	9
2012–	2	1987–	5
2011	3	1986–	3
2010	4	1985–	4
2009–	1	1984–	1
2008	6	1983–	1
2007–	4	1982–	4
2006–	5	1981–	3
2005–	6	1980–	0
2004–	8	1979–	2
2003–	7	1978–	0
2002–	4	1977–	5
2001–	5	1976–	4
2000–	5	1975–	1
1999–	8	1974–	2
1998–	4	1973–	0
1997–	3	1972–	1
1996–	7		
1995–	5		
1994–	4		
1993–	5		
1992–	3		

Table 6.7. Arroyo Wells School District Age of Teachers.

Age	Number	Age	Number
23	0	49	11
24	0	50	10
25	1	51	5
26	3	52	3
27	1	53	4

(Continued)

Table 6.7. Continued

Age	Number	Age	Number
28	2	54	2
29	0	55	4
30	3	56	2
31	2	57	4
32	1	58	2
33	4	59	2
34	5	60	5
35	5	61	0
36	6	62	5
37	7	63	0
38	5	64	0
39	5	65	8
40	5	66	1
41	5	67	2
42	4	68	0
43	4	69	1
44	8		
45	7		
46	2		
47	12		
48	6	All ages are as of June 30, 2016	

DATA ON TEACHERS AGED FIFTY-FIVE AND OLDER

Thirty-six teachers are currently aged fifty-five or older with at least ten years of service in the AWSD.

Number of teachers with a CAGS degree—6
Number of teachers with an EdD./PhD.—3

Table 6.8. Distribution of Teachers by the New England Health Plan.

Plan	Single	Single+1	Family
Dental	6	27	3
PLAN A	1	0	0
PLAN B	1	9	1
PLAN C	4	18	2

(*Continued*)

Chapter 6

Table 6.8. Continued

Age	MA	MA+15	MA+30
55	1		3
56			2
57	1		2
58		1	2
59			1
60		1	5
61			
62			3
63		2	
64			
65			6
66		2	
67		1	2
68			
69			1

BACKUP DATA

Table 6.9. Salaries.

	Arroyo Wells School District				
	Salary Schedule				
Year	BA	BA+15	MA	MA+15	MA+30
1	43,868	46,563	49,923	52,548	56,156
2	44,277	47,226	51,201	54,360	58,237
3	46,156	49,398	53,543	56,867	60,912
4	48,285	51,672	55,670	59,486	63,718
5	50,497	54,047	58,250	62,221	66,643
6	52,820	56,523	60,986	65,143	69,774
7	55,258	59,129	63,858	68,209	73,051
8	57,787	61,849	66,797	71,342	76,421
9	60,454	64,699	69,866	74,627	79,930
10			74,644	79,377	84,531

Education Stipend—Added to Base Salary—Cumulative
CAGS/CAS/EdS.= $1,000
EdD./PhD. = $2,500
Longevity Stipend—Noncumulative

At the start of the twelfth year of service in the AWSD through the fourteenth continuous year of service, a longevity stipend of $1,000 will be awarded.
At the start of the fifteenth year of service in the AWSD through the eighteenth continuous year of service, a longevity stipend of $1,500 will be awarded.
At the start of the nineteenth year of service in the AWSD through the twenty-second continuous year of service, a longevity stipend of $2,000 will be awarded.
At the start of the twenty-fifth year of service and continuing for each continuous year of employment in AWSD, a longevity stipend of $3,000 will be awarded.

Table 6.10. Comparative Salary Schedules.

| | Metroville School District | | | | | |
| | Salary Schedule | | | | | |
Step/Year	BA	BA+15	BA +30	MA	MA+15	MA +30
1	44,900	46,900	48,900			
2	46,550	48,625	50,650	59,650	63,625	67,825
3	48,200	50,350	52,400	61,425	65,425	69,725
4	49,850	52,075	54,150	63,200	67,225	71,625
5	51,500	53,800	55,900	64,975	69,025	73,525
6	53,150	55,525	57,650	66,750	70,825	75,425
7	54,800	57,250	59,400	68,525	72,625	77,325
8	56,450	58,975	61,150	70,300	74,425	79,225
9	58,100	60,700	62,900	72,075	76,225	81,125
10	59,750	62,425	64,650	73,850	78,025	
11	61,400	64,150	66,400	75,625		
12			68,150			
13			69,900			
14			71,650			
15			73,400			

Education Stipend—Added to the Salary Base
EdD./PhD. = $3,000

Longevity Stipend—Added to the Base But Not Cumulative
16–17 years of continuous service in the district = $1,250
18–19 years of continuous service in the district = $1,500
20–29 years of continuous service in the district = $2,000
30+ years of continuous service in the district = $3,000

Table 6.11. Comparative Salary Schedule

| | | Happy Valley School District | | |
| | | Salary Schedule | | |
Years/Step	BA	BA+15	MA	MA+15
1	44,630	46,130		
2	45,905	47,480	58,980	65,000
3	47,180	48,830	61,980	67,000
4	48,455	50,180	63,530	69,000
5	49,730	51,530	65,080	71,500
6	51,005	51,030	66,630	74,000
7	52,280	52,880	68,180	77,000
8	53,555	56,230	69,680	
9	54,830	57,580	72,880	
10	56,105	58,930		
11	57,380	60,630		
12	58,655	62,980		
13		64,330		
14				
15				

Longevity Stipend—The Stipends Are Not Cumulative
16–19 years of continuous service = $1,000
20–22 years of continuous service = $1,500
23+ years of continuous service = $2,000

COMPARATIVE PAY RAISES

Table 6.12. Arroyo Wells and Surrounding School Districts.

Year	Arroyo Wells	Metroville	Happy Valley
This Year	NA	NA	NA
Last Year (%)	3.50	3.25	3.25
Two Years (%)	3.00	3.00	2.75
Three Years (%)	2.75	2.75	2.50

NA: Not Available at this time

Table 6.13. AWSD Scattergram.

Year	BA	BA+15	MA	MA+15	MA+30	TOTAL
1	1					1
2		2				2
3	1	1				2
4	1	1				2
5	1	1				2
6		3				3
7	2	2	2			6
8		1	1			2
9		30	5	5	1	41
10			22	15	77	114
Total	6	41	30	20	78	175
Total Salary	299,322	2,540,215	2,186,011	1,563,790	6,588,817	13,178,155

Education Stipend—Added to Base Salary—Non-Cumulative

CAGS/CAS/EdS. $1,000 (Stipend) × 18 = $18,000
EdD./JD./PhD. $2,500 (Stipend) × 7 = $17,500

Longevity Stipend—Added to Base Salary—Non-Cumulative

12–13 years of continuous service to AWSD: Stipend $1,000 × 14 = $14,000
14–16 years of continuous service to AWSD: Stipend $1,500 × 16 = $24,000
17–19 years of continuous service to AWSD: Stipend $2,000 × 17 = $34,000
20–25 years of continuous service to AWSD: Stipend $2,500 × 27 = $67,500
26+ years of continuous service to AWSD: Stipend $3,000 × 69 = $207,000

Total Stipends = $382,000
Total Salary + Stipends = $13,560,155

Table 6.14. Fringe Benefit Costs.

Plan	Single	Single+1	Family
Monthly Costs (No. of enrollees)			
Dental	32 (34)	67 (62)	110 (79)
Totals per Year	$13,056	$49,848	$104,280
Life Insurance	0.21 per thousand of employee's salary paid by district per year		

Table 6.14. Continued

Plan	Single	Single+1	Family
Total = $2,835			
Disability Insurance	$300 per employee per year paid by the district		
Total = $52,500			

New England Medical Insurers Trust

Plan	Single	Single+1	Family
Plan a Current Monthly	610(4)	920 (9)	1,250 (11)
Total Yearly	$29,280	$99,360	$165,000
Costs for Changes to Plan A			
Plan A $10 Co-pay*	550	800	1,100
• Yearly Deductible**	1,500	1,500	1,500
• Annual Out of Pocket***	3,000	3,000	3,000
Plan	Single	Single+1	Family
Plan B Current	710(8)	1,340 (22)	1,700 (32)
Total Yearly	$68,160	$353,760	$652,800
Costs for Changes to Plan B			
Plan B $10 Co-pay*	615	1,190	1,450
• Yearly Deductible**	500	500	500
• Annual Out of Pocket***	1,000	1,000	1,000
Plan	Single	Single+1	Family
Plan C Current	875(14)	1,450 (31)	2,095 (44)
Total Yearly	$146,000	$539,400	$1,106,160
Costs for Changes to Plan C			
Plan C $10 Co-pay*	760	1,260	1,790
• Yearly Deductible**	200	200	200
• Annual Out of Pocket***	500	500	500

* A $20 dollar co-pay reduces the monthly cost for each of the three categories by 10%. This option does not change yearly deductible or annual out-of-pocket expenses.
** Per person covered, paid before plan begins to pay for share of the cost.
*** Per person covered, limit on the amount paid for covered costs (deductibles and co-pays).

Total Fringe Benefit Costs

Dental Insurance = $167,184

Life Insurance = $2,835

Disability Insurance = $52,500

Medical Insurance = $3,159,920

Grand Total = $3,382,439

AWSD Five-Year Grievance History

This AWSD grievance history tracks those grievances that reached Formal Level One. This history does not track those grievances either withdrawn or resolved at the informal level.

Table 6.15. Grievance Log.

Five Years Ago

Formal Level One

Grievance No.	Issue	Resolution
#01–12	Placement on salary schedule	For employee.
#02–12	Attendance at mandatory	Denied, past practice of requiring
#03–12	department meetings at high	department meetings which are not
#04–12	school (sections 7.3 and 7.7)	faculty meetings.
	Class size at elementary school (section 9.1)	Grievance withdrawn when a student moved out of the class.
	Class size at elementary school (section 9.1)	Grievance withdrawn when a student moved out of the class.

Formal Level Two—Superintendent

Grievance No.	Issue	Resolution
#02–12	Attendance at mandatory department meetings at high school (sections 7.3 and 7.7)	Denied, past practice of requiring department meetings which are not faculty meetings.

Formal Level Three—Advisory Arbitration

Grievance No.	Issue	Resolution
#02–12	Attendance at mandatory department meetings at high school (sections 7.3 and 7.7)	Arbitrator found for grievant citing section 7.3.

Formal Level Four—School Board

Grievance No.	Issue	Resolution
#02–12	Attendance at mandatory department meetings at high school (sections 7.3 and 7.7)	School board overturned arbitrator's decision stating that section 7.7 and past practice were controlling, not section 7.3.

Four Years Ago

Formal Level One

Grievance No.	Issue	Resolution
#01–13	Involuntary reassignment from teaching four eighth-grade history classes and one seventh-grade history class to three eighth-grade history classes and two seventh-grade history classes (section 10.31)	Denied, reassignment not covered in section 10.31, past practice allows management to reassign teaching assignments within the building. Note: In the following year this contract section (10.31) was changed to add the word reassignment. The addition of the language did not reference this grievance.

(Continued)

Table 6.15. Continued

	Three Years Ago	
	No grievances were taken past the informal level	

Two Years Ago

Formal Level One

Grievance No.	Issue	Resolution
#01–15 #02–15	Content of the evaluation (section 12.12b) Derogatory letter from parents was placed in the employee's personnel file without reasonable notice and was used in an evaluation (section 12.2)	Denied, cannot grieve the content of an evaluation. All procedures of section 12.12 were followed. Section 12.12(e) is controlling. Denied, citing section 12.12(c) that letter was not hearsay and section 12.12(e) cannot grieve substance of evaluation.

Formal Level Two—Superintendent

Grievance No.	Issue	Resolution
#02–15	Derogatory letter from parents was placed in the employee's personnel file without reasonable notice and was used in an evaluation (section 12.2)	Denied, citing section 12.12(c) that letter was not hearsay and section 12.12(e) cannot grieve substance of evaluation.

Formal Level Three—Advisory Arbitration

Grievance No.	Issue	Resolution
#02–15	Derogatory letter from parents was placed in the employee's personnel file without reasonable notice and was used in an evaluation (section 12.2)	Accepted, citing that employee did not receive timely notice of the derogatory letter from parents in a reasonable or timely manner. Therefore, the employee never had the opportunity to provide a response. Section 12.2 controlling, content of evaluation must only use information appropriately gathered.

Formal Level Four—School Board

Grievance No.	Issue	Resolution
#02–15	Derogatory letter from parents was placed in the employee's personnel file without reasonable notice and was used in an evaluation (section 12.2)	Accepted arbitrator's decision. Derogatory letter expunged and evaluation withdrawn. Evaluation must be rewritten without the use of derogatory letter.

(Continued)

Table 6.15. Continued

Last Year

Formal Level One

Grievance No.	Issue	Resolution
#01–16	Class size at elementary	Withdrawn when a student left the
#02–16	school (section 9.1)	classroom.
#03–16	Class size at elementary	Denied, citing section 9.63, exploring
#04–16	school (section 9.1)	possible alternatives.
#05–16	Class size at elementary	Withdrawn when a student left the
	school (section 9.1)	classroom.
	Faculty meeting at high	Denied. Faculty meeting started fifteen
	school went fifteen	minutes late because faculty came to
	minutes over the one-	the meeting late.
	hour limit (section 7.3)	Denied, citing section 9.63, exploring
	Class size at elementary	possible alternatives.
	school (section 9.1)	

Formal Level Two—Superintendent

Grievance No.	Issue	Resolution
#02–16	Class size at elementary	Resolved when additional students
#05–16	school (section 9.1)	moved into school, which resulted in
	Class size at elementary	establishment of a combination grade.
	school (section 9.1)	Denied but was later withdrawn before
		advisory arbitration hearing.

Letter of Interest for AWTA Bargaining Team

(Restricted to Union Team)

TO: AWTA Bargaining Team
FR: TAD, President
RE: Expedited Bargaining

I know that you have begun the process of preparing for our two-day expedited bargaining sessions in an effort to settle the contract or declare impasse. I want to restate our interests as you continue your preparations. Our interests should guide your actions at the table. If you are unclear about any proposals potentially running counter to our interests, please contact me right away. I am also available should you need information or want to discuss strategies.

SALARY AND FRINGE BENEFITS

Salary is an obvious interest of ours. We want to be paid the best wage that we can, given the important and vital professional service that we render to the community. We must also be realistic as to the reasonableness of our salary demands. We want a competitive wage that attracts new teachers and retains experienced teachers.

The maintenance of needed fringe benefits is important. Unfortunately, we are facing a dilemma. The costs of fringe benefits are escalating at an alarming rate and have been doing so for a number of years. This is a challenge not only for the district but for us as well. We have reached the point where the new available monies going into the maintenance of our extraordinary benefit package—which, by the way, we are quite proud of the fact that we have negotiated a package that is the envy of surrounding school districts—is starting to erode the salary increases.

It is in our best interests not to let the balance of salary and benefits shift too far out of balance. We can posture publicly as much as we want about how the district must pay for both and that the costs of increased insurance premiums should not be placed on the backs of hardworking teachers. However, the Association leadership is concerned that the reality of financing public schools and the uncontrolled costs of rising medical and dental insurance have forced us into a position that 100 percent district-paid benefits may no longer be sustainable.

If necessary, explore options that mitigate the impact of this potential burden-shifting. If we give something on fringe we need to get something in return that we can sell to our constituency. If you can gain an additional year or two before implementation of a cost-sharing proposal that would serve our members in the short run and provide for a better balance in the long run.

The issue of a freeze on salary movement and access to early retirement based on a Remediation Plan presents us with a conundrum. If we oppose we look like we support incompetence. If we agree, will our membership believe they have been abandoned? We will need to agree some form of this language, but try to mitigate the expansion of it. Develop a tight response that supports professional practice with a buffer so that it cannot be used as a cudgel. Possibly consider leveraging this to change Evaluations 12(e).

The issue of increasing the compensation for unused sick leave is something that many of our older members are interested in as they near retirement. The younger members are not as interested and don't want to lose something important to get it. Anything that we can that increases compensation is good, but we don't want to give up a more important interest such as salary, professionalism, and arbitration.

PROFESSIONAL RESPONSIBILITIES

We want to enhance our professional status, if possible. We look at professionalism as having more control over our time and manageable class size. Even if the research does not support a small reduction in class size, we definitely do not want an increase.

Related to professional status is section 7.7 on professional responsibilities. This has been a thorn in our side even though management has been circumspect in its use. It could, however, expand and place more control over our time in the hands of management. Try to get a modification of the language limiting its reach. It is important that we get our position on the table for future negotiations. We must continue to push against this even though not getting a change is not a deal-breaker for us. Failure to get a change does not trigger a BATNA (Best Alternative to a Negotiated Agreement).

REASSIGNMENT

The issue of reassignment can be a troubling one for us. If we sacrifice flexibility for a rigid seniority of reassignments we will bounce our members through the schools. This is a battle that we don't want to take on because it would be a battle within our membership. We can defend seniority as a basis for transfers but it is a less potent argument in face of large movements of teachers. If we can get the district to buy into the notion of school-level seniority it may be more palatable for our members. Getting rid of reassignment in this section transfers is important to the district. If we can't get school level seniority to govern reassignment, try to get something for eliminating it from the section. However, we must keep district seniority for transfers between schools.

BINDING ARBITRATION

Binding arbitration is a big deal. The members want the sense of fairness that comes with binding arbitration. Similarly, the ability to grieve the content of an observation and or evaluation would be a great win. This is high on our list of interests.

EARLY RETIREMENT

A number of our more senior members are clamoring for an early retirement package. It is in our best interests to get the best deal that we can.

These interests should guide your actions at the table. It is important that you keep me apprised as to your progress.

Solidarity!

Letter of Interest for School District Bargaining Team

(Restricted to Management Team)

TO: District Bargaining Team
FR: Dr. Oz, Arroyo Wells School District Superintendent
RE: Bargaining Interests

As you prepare for our ten hours of expedited bargaining in an effort to settle the contract I want to share with you the interests that you are to pursue at the bargaining table. We have six major interests.

First, because of budget concerns we must hold the line on increasing our ongoing expenditures. Proposals that increase ongoing salary commitments beyond where we currently are in negotiations and without a short-term or long-term improvement in the budget must be avoided.

- Class size is a salary issue as well as an instructional issue. If we lower class size we will incur more costs not just for the addition of the teacher but at the elementary school level to support the 300 minutes of release time every ten school days. We will have to add additional faculty as we increase the number of elementary school teachers. We are not seeking to change the 300 minutes of preparation time for elementary school teachers. However, if we can reduce the number of students from two to one for section 9.2 combination classes that will assist our cost-cutting as well. We need to explore options about what to do when we cannot reduce the size of a class when it violates the class size section of the contract. We need flexibility.
- Salary increases must be held down. Any offer above the 1 percent on the table must show cost savings in other areas—fringe benefits, class size, early retirement are possible cost saving measures. Paid leaves and changes to the extra duty stipend also impact the salary budget line. If you increase

the salary budget line, you must demonstrate a savings in some other budget line.

An important part of the compensation package is the new language on freezing salary schedule movement. This is not a cost item for us. It is a professional position—we cannot reward a teacher with additional pay when their work is not satisfactory. We took a beating in the community when it became known that one of our teachers who was on a remediation plan for incompetence received both a horizontal and vertical raise, separate from a cost-of-living raise that changed the salary schedule. We have not had a problem with the early retirement portion of the new language, but I believe, as does the school board, that it cuts from the same cloth. We must get something that supports professional service.

Second, we need to move from the 100 percent paid benefits. This has long-term disastrous consequences for the budget. The more money that we pour into premium costs reduces the amount of money available for other competing demands including salary. It is in our best interests, and I believe the best interests of our teachers, to get a handle on these escalating costs through some form of burden-sharing. Either a dollar cap on benefits that the district pays or a percentage sharing plan will meet our interests. We must achieve some burden-sharing when it comes to health benefits; otherwise, it will eat up any raises that our faculty deserve but we will not be able to provide.

Because this is such an important issue we will probably need to make sure that the teachers are held harmless with no increase for at least one year, maybe two at the most. One way to do that is to raise the cap to a level that no individual teacher will have any out-of-pocket expenses for at least one or two years. If you bargain a percentage you can look at an off-the-salary schedule mitigation for one year or two years maximum. This mitigation would involve a set dollar amount that equals the differential between the 100 percent and the reduced percentage the district pays. This amount would not go on the salary schedule and would be issued as a one-time bonus.

An increase of compensation for unused sick leave could be worthwhile if it encourages teachers to be more judicious in the use of sick leave. Any increase in the amount of minimum compensation should be balanced with an increase in the percentage of unused sick leave that can be exchanged for compensation. Be open to creative solutions to decrease the use of sick leave, thus saving it for truly needy situations. There may be win-win potential options for both sides.

Three, we need to change 10.3. The word reassignment must come out. We need the flexibility to reassign teachers within a building without this convoluted movement necessitated by bumping through the schools based on district seniority. While this is very important to us, I am concerned about setting a precedent in which we trade language for money.

Four, an early retirement package would be nice and would serve our interests *only* if we can show that it saved the district money over a five-year period. We cannot give money away to employees who would retire anyway. We must find the sweet spot where the incentive is enough to induce someone to take the package now in case it will not be available in the future.

Five, while binding arbitration is a political issue. The school board sees it as an infringement on its power and does not want a third party to make decisions that they believe infringe on their discretion. However, the movement is toward decisions (and consistent with federal NLRB decisions) that a CBA must have a workable grievance process, which has been considered as ending in binding arbitration. We can give on this but only if we get significant concessions on fringe benefit burden-sharing and do not reduce our ability to effectively manage the school district. Any considerations of binding arbitration must include a discussion of positive assurance to protect our interests on what is arbitrable.

Six, section 7.7 is one that the AWTA wants to change. It has worked well for us. It gives us flexibility. It is very important that we keep this flexibility. Without it we may find ourselves in a situation in which every activity that has not been spelled out explicitly in the contract results in a change in past practice and an occasion to renegotiate additional stipends and hourly rates. This is important.

You represent the school district, its community, and the students. Be willing to play hardball if called for, but as we have discussed let's keep grounded in the concepts of *Getting to Together* and *Getting to Yes*. We must work with the teachers after bargaining. We do not want our bargaining to resemble General Sherman's march to Atlanta, we win but destroy everything in our path. The teachers are our colleagues and not an enemy or an obstacle. Please keep me up to date after each meeting. If you are concerned that a specific proposal may violate our interests, you must talk to me right away.

Best wishes on your bargaining. Our students and community rely on and trust your good judgment and your commitment to strengthening our school district through working collaboratively with our teachers at and beyond the bargaining table.

Early Bargaining Letters to Bargaining Teams

These letters are sent to the union and management teams as means to orient them to the bargaining tasks ahead.

UNION BARGAINING TEAM LETTER

Joe, Stefanie, TeShawn, Paul, Fatima, and Joy,

Thank you for your willingness to serve on our bargaining team and to represent the 175 teachers of the AWSD. This is a critically important task and one that requires the hard work of dedicated educators. I wish that I could say that there are great rewards associated with serving on the bargaining, but I can't. No laurels are handed out and instead we are criticized. But I think that is born from the importance of the job and the impact that it has on the lives of our colleagues.

Expedited bargaining will be starting soon. You will need to be prepared. I have provided documents on where bargaining left off and what were the latest positions. I have also included in the documents the interests of the union and the educators we serve. This will provide a compass for you as you bargain for our interests. I will also be available to assist at any time. The strategies that you will use are primarily yours to develop; the interests that you pursue are all of ours. Remember, this is not about you, it is about the educators we serve.

I understand that you will have a session in two weeks to review where we are in bargaining. Both our team and management's team are all new. Dr. Oz and I agreed to each select a totally new team so that each can bring fresh eyes to the expedited bargaining and not be burdened by prior bargaining. Once bargaining starts, it will go fast. The two meetings of five hours each seems like a lot but it isn't. We need to be prepared.

I have great confidence in you. Jacob and I would not have asked you to serve if we had any reservations. Please let Jacob or me know if you have any questions. Once again, many thanks.

Best,

TAD

President, AWTA

Fifth Grade Teacher, Main Street School

Jacob A. Bennett

Negotiations Chair, AWTA

English Teacher, Arroyo Wells High School

MANAGEMENT BARGAINING TEAM LETTER

Maryann, Ricardo, Jovana, Matthew, Justin, and Te-Hsin,

Thank you for your willingness to serve on the district bargaining team. You are representing the school district, and perhaps, more importantly, the students and community that we serve. We realize that this is an additional task that is being added to your already crowded "to do" list. But your perspective, experience, sense of fairness, and acceptance of responsibility will serve you and your constituency well.

You will soon start two five-hour sessions of bargaining. Dr. Evans and I have developed the letter of interests that will guide your expedited bargaining. As you know, the AWTA leadership team and the district management team decided that we would each seat new bargaining teams so as to provide fresh eyes on the issues that separate our two sides. You will sit on the opposite side of the table from colleagues for bargaining, but will join with them in providing the best education that we can for our students and community.

We will be available to assist in any way that we can. Please know that we appreciate your willingness to serve on this very important task.

I have great confidence in you. Jacob and I would not have asked you to serve if we had any reservations. Please let Jacob or me know if you have any questions. Once again, many thanks.

Regards,

Dr. Oz

Superintendent of Schools

Arroyo Wells School District

Carla M. Evans, PhD

Associate Superintendent of Curriculum and Assessment

About the Author

Todd A. DeMitchell is the John and H. Irene Peters professor of education and professor of justice studies at the University of New Hampshire. He teaches courses on labor relations, school law, and education policy. Prior to joining the faculty at the University of New Hampshire, he served for eighteen years as an elementary school teacher (grades 4, 5, and 6), principal (K–8), director of personnel and labor relations (K–12), and superintendent (K–8). He sat at the bargaining table representing two school districts. He studied collective bargaining at the University of Southern California (doctorate) and at Harvard University (post-doctorate). He has published seven books—five published by Rowman & Littlefield Publishers. His publications with Rowman & Littlefield include *The Challenges of Mandating School Uniforms in the Public Schools: Free Speech, Research, and Policy* (2015) with Richard Fossey; *Student Dress Codes and the First Amendment: Legal Challenges and Policy Issues* (2014) with Richard Fossey; *Labor Relations in Education: Policies, Politics, and Practices* (2010); *Negligence: What Principals Need to Know about Avoiding Liability* (2006); and *The Limits of Law-Based School Reform: Vain Hopes and False Promises* (1997) with Richard Fossey. He has published more than 200 book chapters and articles in law reviews, peer-reviewed journals, professional journals, and other venues. His research has been cited in major law reviews, in peer-reviewed journals, and by state and federal courts.